100 Ideas for Teaching Creative Development

Continuum One Hundreds Series

100 Ideas for Teaching

Creative
Development

Stephen Bowkett and
Wendy Bowkett

continuum

Continuum International Publishing Group

The Tower Building	80 Maiden Lane
11 York Road	Suite 704
London	New York
SE1 7NX	NY 10038

www.continuumbooks.com

British Library Cataloguing-in-Publication Data
A catalogue record for this book is available from the British Library.

ISBN: 9-780-8264-9929-5 (paperback)

Designed and typeset by Kenneth Burnley, Wirral, Cheshire
Printed and bound in Great Britain by Antony Rowe Ltd

Contents

Section 2: Listening, Sounds and Music

Section 3: Imagination, Words and Feelings

Acknowledgements

I have met many people who influenced my attitude to education. My mum's voice through poetry, stories and love, my brothers and sister through playing together, children, parents and colleagues I've met in schools. My dad called it The Wendy Way. I would like to acknowledge all these people, but especially Warwick, Matthew and Rory who have no idea how positively they affected my career. Also thanks to Jane, Breda and Christine, Fiona, Cheryl and Julie – very special colleagues I had the pleasure of working with. Without my husband though, this book would never have been written, so thank you Steve.

Wendy Bowkett

The great comedian Bob Monkhouse said that growing old is compulsory but growing up is optional. My thanks to all the people who have helped me keep a childlike heart throughout my career in education. And, to Wendy, my love and deepest respect for all she has taught me about learning.

Steve Bowkett

Health and Safety Note

We advise that all of the activities in this book be carried out under adult supervision, with the art activities especially being closely supervised. As a pre-school practitioner you know your children and should judge which ones are capable of doing which activities for themselves, or where and how much adult help with equipment is needed. Wear protective clothing such as apron and gloves when handling dyes, etc. Do not allow children to use irons. If using sprays ensure windows are open. Be aware of children with allergies and asthma when using paints, fibres, chalk and sand, etc.

Introduction

The Russian psychologist Lev Vygotsky once said that the greatest achievements are possible in play, and that 'Play is the realm of spontaneity and freedom'. This is a view shared by Sue Palmer in her influential book *Toxic Childhood*, where she asserts that symbolic play – i.e. play through the active use of the imagination – has been significant throughout history in developing children's creativity and problem-solving skills.

It is our firm belief, supported by vast research in neuroscience and other fields, that all children are born creative. At its most fundamental creativity is a survival skill, because it leads to flexibility of thinking and adaptability of response in a changing world. And the modern world is changing more quickly than ever before. The whole 'learning to learn' movement hinges on the development of children's creativity and of their ability to think for themselves.

This is a process that must lie at the heart of all children's experience in preschool. Cultivating natural curiosity, valuing ideas, developing empathy and the ability to communicate thoughts constitute the creative attitude that we advocate throughout this book. Creative play embodies the attributes, skills and qualities that are the vital precursors to the more sophisticated and academically rigorous learning children will undertake later in their education.

In preparing this book we have of course been aware of the Government's Early Learning Goals (ELGs) and the educational structure that lies behind them. Our ideas are fully congruent with the ELGs: but we suggest that such goals can only be fully realized within the field of play.

Section 1:
Media and Materials

Colour Naming

Helping children to identify and name basic colours is a precursor to having them work with colour in more sophisticated and varied ways. Make sure there is a range of different colours in the room for visual reference as you talk about colours. Build colour-related words into your conversations with the children: 'I love that blue top you're wearing, Nathan'; 'Emily, your hairband is a much brighter red than mine'; 'See how the leaves of this tree are a lighter green than the grass'; 'Look how many kinds of blue there are in the sky . . .'

Here are some ideas for making colour naming fun.

- Use rhyme to familiarize children with a variety of colours – and be creative yourself in adapting well-known rhymes for this purpose. So, for example, to the tune of 'Ten green bottles', sing: 'There are three yellow beanbags lying on the chair . . . And if one yellow beanbag suddenly wasn't there we'd see two yellow beanbags lying on the chair.' Add enjoyment to the song by actually putting out three (or however many) yellow beanbags and having a different child each time remove one. When all the beanbags are gone, do the song in reverse and have children replace them on the chair. Change the colours of the bags or put a variety of coloured beanbags on the chair and sing each colour separately so that each child has to differentiate one colour from the others.

- Kim's Game. Prepare a tray holding a number of identical objects of different colours. The children close their eyes. Take an object away and ask the children which colour is now missing.

- Colour Trays. Have a number of plastic trays, each of a different colour. On the red tray place lots of red objects, etc. Use this technique for developing children's use of colour adjectives such as reddish, light blue, chestnut brown and so on.

IDEA 2

Shades and Hues

The naming of colours is basic to the development of any child's vocabulary and perception of the world (see Ideas 1 and 3). Extend this work by obtaining paint colour charts from DIY stores (such samplers are usually free).

- Use these to help the children extend their vocabulary and discriminate between a range of different hues.

- Have the children mix paints to try and reproduce some of the colours on the charts, adding small amounts at a time to see subtle colour changes. Remember to add dark to light: lighter added to darker will only result in a 'muddy' mess.

- Work with the children to invent new colour names along the same lines as those found on the samplers. A simple version of this is to use the names of animals, objects and materials and to turn their names into descriptions, for example chestnut brown, grassy green, sky blue, daffodil yellow. Extend this work by comparing items showing different hues and shades of the same basic colour – grassy green and lime green for instance. Depending on the children's abilities, encourage them to explain the differences between the greens in greater or lesser detail.

- Notice too how colours are not always described using purely visual references. We might speak of gloomy grey, zesty orange, earthy brown, warm red, cool blue, etc. In other words, colours can be associated with moods and feelings, touch, texture and temperature, taste and smell and even sounds.

This is one aspect of a phenomenon called *synaesthesia*, a blending of the senses in perception which in some individuals is so strong that they might actually hallucinate colours upon hearing sounds, or taste different flavours when they look at various colours. For most people synaesthesia exists more in the imagination and the way we use language: colours and moods for example are commonly blended (green with envy, feeling blue, etc).

 Taking this further

For more on this, see *100 Ideas for Teaching Creativity* by Stephen Bowkett (Idea 63 The Colour of Saying).

Changing Colours

As children become more able to identify and name an increasing range of colours, challenge them further in a variety of ways. Note that these sessions need only last a few minutes, but this is enough to help children to begin to play with colour-related concepts and objects.

- Use colour lenses and encourage children to look through them, for example at the cut-out white shape of a bird or a white toy polar bear. Start with one colour, then progress to two colours that don't naturally blend (so not blue and yellow for example). Use the experience to help children understand that the lenses change their perception of things. The polar bear is still a polar bear, but each change of colour introduces an obvious difference. (Tip: Colour lenses can be made very cheaply by using coloured perspex stuck to a cardboard frame. Tissue paper is even cheaper and objects can be seen through it in a good light; or use coloured cellophane from sweet wrappers.)

- Use colour lenses that *do* blend. Allow children to discover for themselves that, for instance, red and yellow make orange. (You have of course set up your room so that such discoveries are pretty likely if not inevitable. This strategy is called the 'principle of the controlled accident'. The children discover what you intended them to, but have that wonderful sense that the discovery was their own.)

- Use stencils to create shapes on white paper. Let the children tear little pieces of coloured tissue paper to stick on the outlines using a thin adhesive. As paper pieces overlap they can form new colours.

Soaking Up Colours

- Add primary coloured ink or food colouring to a jar of water, and then place a white carnation with a short stem in the jar. Over the course of a few hours capillary action will draw the coloured water into the flower's petals, making complex and delicate patterns. The stronger the mix of colour to water, the deeper the colours that are taken up.

- Following on from this, gently split the lower part of the stem in half and put one half of the stem in one glass of primary coloured water and the other half in a glass of another primary colour. Notice the dual colouration over time.

- Use different primary coloured inks, dyes and food colouring for varying effects and try with different strengths of coloured water to make deeper-coloured flowers.

- Try splitting the stem three ways and use primary colours only for more complex effects.

- Experiment with non-primary colours and notice effects. Look closely at what happens when green dye is used – the colour separates into blue and yellow through the veins in the flower petals. What happens if you use two non-primary colours with a split-stem flower?

- What happens with a four-way split stem?

IDEA

5

Gritty Colours

This is a variation on using glitter to make pictures. You will need sand, paint (ready mixed or powder), bowls for mixing, pieces of wood, thick sugar paper or cardboard, white glue and brushes.

- Mix sand and paint (adding water if using powder paint) and stir well so that all the grains of sand are coloured. Let the sand dry thoroughly, then put each colour in a separate container.

- Draw a picture or pattern on the piece of wood, cardboard or thick sugar paper and then decide which colour to make each section. The children can help with this.

- Brush glue (not too thickly) onto one area at a time, and sprinkle on the sand with a spoon or paper cone. Excess sand can be tapped from the card onto a sheet of paper and returned to its appropriate container. Allow each area of sand to dry before adding the next colour. Experiment for best effects.

This idea of 'colouring' textures can be tried with wood shavings, cotton yarn, crushed eggshells, melon seeds, lollipop sticks, etc. to create a huge variety of colour-and-texture experiences for the children.

Colour Blending

You will need wax crayons (to save using good or new crayons, use broken, old or 'mottled' ones), plain paper, plenty of newspaper, an iron and an ironing board.

Prepare for this activity by grating some wax crayons. Fold the sheet of paper in half, open it back out and sprinkle shavings of different wax crayon colours on to the paper. Now fold the paper again and cover the sheet with several layers of newspaper (which draws out the oil and leaves less on the child's picture). Heat gently with a warm iron to melt the shavings, thus blending the coloured waxes together (we strongly recommend that only an adult should handle the hot iron).

Rainbow Weaving

For this activity use strips of rainbow-coloured paper. These can be bought or painted: bought paper chains are ideal, but if using painted papers, they will need to be dried beforehand and then cut into strips.

● Children create rainbow strips for themselves using paints or wax crayons by carefully choosing the colours they'll use to match the rainbow template you prepared earlier. Help the children to line up their rainbow strips so that all the reds, oranges, yellows, etc. match as closely as possible.

● Play with rainbows. Get the children to deliberately mismatch their strips to create a more complex mosaic effect.

● Progress to rainbow weaving. Take around six rainbow strips. Stick the ends of each strip to a piece of card so that they form the warp (aligned lengthwise), then using other strips weave under and over. Use different widths of warp or weft (crosswise strips) to create a multicoloured braid, or even taper the strips to make thin isosceles triangles for a different effect. Demonstrate this technique to the children then help them to try for themselves, using the rainbow strips they created earlier.

● There is no right or wrong outcome to these activities – all results will be colourful, individual and unique.

IDEA

8

Outside Weaving

Prepare for this activity by driving sticks or posts into the ground, or use traffic cones with poles through the centres. Give the children ropes, wool, ribbon, paper, etc. and show them how to weave them in and out of the sticks.

● Experiment with different colours and thicknesses of paper.

● Use different patterns – rather than weaving in and out alternately, weave in and out of the sticks two at a time, or try a one–two pattern. Look at the different effects that are created and discuss the differences in patterning.

● Extend the activity into a group game or movement activity. Draw chalk markings, put beanbags or blocks on the ground and have the children weave in and out. How fast can they complete the course (use a timer or count)?

● Move the beanbags closer to each other: is it harder or easier to weave?

● Increase the challenge by having the children interweave 'military tattoo-style', criss-crossing two lines. This takes concentration, varying speed and careful attention by each child to what all the others are doing.

IDEA 9

Symmetry

Symmetry is the dividing of a shape in such a way that the parts match and balance. In that sense it is an aspect of geometry. But the word also refers to a 'sense' of symmetry, an aesthetic appreciation of balance, proportion and harmony of form. Exploring symmetry in simple ways with the children acts as a precursor to the development of both kinds of understanding.

- Show the children in very basic ways how symmetry works. Use simple shapes like circles, equilateral triangles and squares; fold them over so that the halves overlap exactly. Point out that the halves match, whereas with other (asymmetrical) shapes halves or parts cannot be made to match.

- Point out symmetry in the natural world. Use a paper cut-out human figure and show how this can be folded over so that one half covers the other. Unfold the shape to show the line of symmetry (the dividing line). This is bilateral symmetry. Explain to the children that most people's bodies are the same on the left side as on the right side. Show other examples like birds and butterflies. Show children pictures of starfish, which display a more complex symmetry (radial symmetry), with the matching segments radiating from a central point.

- Combine an exploration of symmetry with colour work. Fold a sheet of paper in two, then open it back out. Have the child splash, paint and/or sprinkle coloured inks or paints on to one half of the sheet of paper, then refold and rub gently all over the folded paper so that the inkblots are reproduced. Open out the sheet and allow it to dry.

IDEA

10

String Pictures

Prepare for this activity by cutting enough lengths of string so that each child involved has three or four lengths to use. Fold sheets of paper in half, open back out and give each child a sheet. The children dip a length of their string into coloured inks or paint and then lay the string carefully onto their sheets, with the 'undipped' end of the string sticking out. Refold the sheet: with one hand holding the folded paper quite firmly, get the children to pull the string out. (A sheet of thick cardboard or sheets of newspaper placed over the top of the picture and held down when pulling out the string helps younger children.)

Unfold the sheets and either allow to dry, or the children can add another colour to their picture immediately. The colours will blend in different ways depending on the degree of dryness of the paint or inks. The pictures can be built up by repeating the activity using other colours.

Top Tips!

Drying racks are really useful for this and many other paint or ink-based activities, but they do take up a fair amount of space, at least tabletop size. If you don't have a drying rack, dry pictures flat on tables or floor, as hanging causes the liquid to run and alters the finished result.

IDEA 11

Folded Paper Shapes

Prepare enough paper shapes so that each child can have several goes at this activity. Shapes can be bought at some art and craft stores, and this saves a great deal of time. Alternatively use stencils or templates created on a computer – in Microsoft Word for instance there is an Autoshapes tool. Clicking on this will bring up a selection of basic shapes. These can be manipulated and copied very easily, and the file printed and saved.

● Show the children how a folded paper circle can make, for example, a tortoise. Depending on the children's abilities they can cut out, fold, draw and colour their own, or you may need to prepare templates for them simply to colour or embellish with fabric, feathers or papers. Most animals can be drawn very simply using the body as a semicircle with legs, head and tail added in the appropriate places on the outline; or use the semi-circle for the head only.

● Extend the technique by working with the children to make 'rocking cards', which are made as above with a circle folded to make a semicircle that forms the base of the card. These can then be embellished with tissue paper, sequins, ribbon pieces, sweet papers, etc. Shapes can be added to the folded edge to change the outline and balance of the card. Add glitter, sequins or other finishing touches and then write your message.

IDEA 12

Concertina Folding

A more sophisticated kind of paper folding is concertina work. Most children over four years old will enjoy the experience of folding paper in concertina style. Younger children may need folded strips prepared for them.

- Make a concertina person using a circular body and two concertina arms and legs attached at appropriate points. Add cut-out feet and hands and a circular head with wool for hair to complete the effect. Obviously these people can be made more elaborate, depending on the age, ability or creativity of the child. Clothes can be designed, hair and headwear added, and shoes, scarves, etc. introduced.

- A jumping jack in a box is made using a concertina strip that fits into a matchbox or similar. Once a head has been drawn and added and the body decorated, glue the other end of the concertina into the matchbox, fold the 'jack' away and carefully close the box. When the box is opened Jack will jump out. Adapt this idea to make a frog, monster, etc. Children love this activity because the finished product makes people jump!

- Use lollipop sticks to create crocodiles, Chinese dragons, lions and other creatures. Once the paper length is decorated and folded concertina-style add a lollipop stick to each end so that by moving the sticks the concertina 'comes to life' and dances. Add a head and tail as necessary to make the required animal and you have a simple stick puppet.

- Make a fan with lollipop sticks and concertina-folded sheets. Use a square or rectangular piece of paper rather than long thin strips, then decorate (perhaps using punch type cutters along the top edge to allow air to flow through the holes when the fan is waved). Concertina in the usual way. Stick the bottom end folds together with tape, peg or ribbon secured around the base. The fan is then opened out and ready for use.

Join-the-dots Games

There are many join-the-dots books of varying complexity available. Use these to develop the children's understanding of ordinal numbering and recognition of numerals. Subsequently you can build on this work in more creative ways.

- Children can create a few dots on a piece of paper for themselves, and then join them up. This may result in a recognizable object or just be an abstract picture, which can be subsequently coloured and decorated.

- Children can create a page of different-coloured dots. They then join the dots of the same colour to create patterns, or join the dots in alternating colours for different effects.

- Create a page of dots of the same or different colours then swap with a friend to join them up.

- Any simple drawing the child has done can be made into a dot-to-dot puzzle. Use tracing paper clipped to the original drawing and carefully place dots to pick out the shapes. Whether these dots are numbered depends on the ability of the child. When the original picture is taken away you are left with the numbered outline. Sometimes part of the outline needs to be drawn alongside the dots. Give the dots puzzle to another child and see if they create a 'copy' of the original or make the dots into a different pattern or picture. This allows children to begin to understand that different people see the world in different ways, and that shapes can be interpreted variously.

Wax Scratch

All you need for this are ordinary wax crayons, paper and a pointed marker (which can be a stick, matchstick or the end of a paintbrush).

● Choose a coloured crayon and rub the flat side of the crayon over the paper: you need to rub hard for the best effects. Add more colours as you want, colouring randomly over the paper leaving as little white space as possible. Your paper should end up covered with different colours.

● Take the black crayon and rub *all* over the colours until the whole sheet of paper is covered in black.

● Now you are ready to create a picture. With the pointed end of your 'brush' scratch through the black surface to reveal the different colours underneath. Use this technique to create abstracts, mosaic patterns and tessellations.

Try using a different colour as the 'top coat', or only one or two background colours to create different effects. Talk about how the background picture changes with a different-coloured foreground: which do the children prefer visually?

Magic Painting

For this activity you need a selection of colour washes (which can be made with coloured inks or food colouring in water, or watery paint), a white wax crayon or non-coloured candle, white painting paper and brushes of varying thicknesses. Magic painting is best done on a flat surface to prevent the colour wash 'running down' the picture as it is created – unless the child wants to create that particular effect.

Initially a child can just 'take the crayon or candle for a walk' and continue to 'draw' until either the child feels he or she has 'done enough' or, without lifting the crayon or candle, he or she reaches the starting point again. Then using one or more colour washes the child paints over the paper, revealing their 'magic' picture.

There is a delightful element of surprise to this activity. Once you start drawing with the crayon or candle it is very difficult to see where you've been, and therefore the results can be startling – once the colour wash is lightly painted over the paper the 'magic' picture appears, as the paint does not stick to the wax. Exploit this by drawing pictures, patterns or the children's names on the sheets yourself, so that the child has no idea as to what will be revealed.

Top Tips! **You can guide the child's 'route' around the paper by first drawing a light pencil line yourself.**

Marbling with Marbles

You will need ready-mixed paint in tubes, marbles, rollers (smooth ones are best for this activity), paper and a shallow dish or bowl large enough for your chosen-sized piece of paper. Have a bowl of water close by for 'finger dipping' to clean off excess paint.

Marbling can be difficult for younger children to do on their own, so two simpler activities can be used with them to achieve a random effect.

- Place paper in the tray. Drop a marble into the paint, and cover it with as much or as little paint as required.

- Lift the marble out and place it into the tray, then tilt the tray backwards and forwards, or jiggle the tray so that as the marble rolls over the paper it leaves swirling lines behind. Repeat the process several times with the same or different colours. Experiment with different thicknesses of paint for other effects.

- Allow the work to dry on a flat surface. Subsequently use it as an opportunity to talk with the children about why the ball sometimes runs fast, sometimes slow, what the picture reminds them of, etc.

- Alternatively: pour paint onto a smooth roller in a random pattern to create thin lines. Move it all over the paper, rolling in different directions to create a marbled effect. More than one colour can be used on the roller at a time, and this creates blends of colour within the picture.

IDEA 17

More Marbling

Develop these techniques by using marbling inks or paints, which are readily obtainable. Some marbling inks are water-resistant for use on fabrics that can be washed without losing the pattern; others are purely for creative purposes. Preparation is simple, the activity is swift and the effects can be stunning. Every picture will be unique and almost impossible to recreate.

- Prepare a tray containing some water. Each child carefully places little drops of the marbling ink on the water's surface, then lightly swirls with a stick to create patterns. Hold opposite corners of a sheet of paper and place it gently on top of the water (the gentler you are, the less air bubbles there'll be to spoil the pattern). Lift the sheet from the water and place flat to dry: using a drying rack is best, but otherwise a tabletop covered in newspaper to absorb excess water will work just as well. You may need to change the water in the tray after each child has had a go, depending on how much ink or paint was used.

- Try dipping polystyrene shapes onto the surface for different effects.

- Dip fabric by holding opposite corners and lowering gently onto the water. Lift almost immediately for best results.

IDEA

18

Finger Painting

Like rollering this can be a messy activity, so cover work surfaces with paper. Also make sure there are handwashing facilities *in the room*; if you do not have a sink then use several bowls and be prepared to change the water in these often.

To minimize mess and waste, use small amounts of paint in palette trays and initially apply paint to the children's fingers yourself with a brush, or allow them to dip their fingertips into the required colour. Explain that the idea is to mix the colours on the paper with their fingers and to keep the colours separate in the palette trays, so to use a different fingertip for each colour.

The thickness of the blobs of paint on the children's fingers will affect the result of each picture and will encourage experimentation with shapes and patterns. The emphasis is on playful exploration, so there should be no pressure to produce finished pictures or recognizable shapes at the outset. The children will inevitably learn that varying the thickness of paint on the fingers and different hand movements and techniques will produce various effects.

Develop the activity by:

- Putting a different colour of paint on each finger. Rehearse colour matching and naming by asking a child to make a blue streak, a red blob, a green patch, etc. This simple game also serves to develop children's fine motor skills and coordination.

- Limiting the range of colours available. Having just blue and white or red and white for example will also produce pleasing results, and helps children to learn the value of simplicity in art.

- Using just thumb prints, add a blob on the print for an eye; introduce a zigzag mark at one side and two lines with three prongs and there's a little bird . . . Develop the idea to make a cat, dog, etc.

Handy Printing Tips

Printing of any kind allows children to learn about and experiment with colour and shape. You can 'max up' from finger painting to hand printing, which also calls for manual dexterity and results in some spectacular results and impressively large pictures.

- Mount several cut-out handprints to represent hedgehogs or owls, etc., with eyes and feet added if necessary. There are lots of opportunities for making ordinary prints into animals or pictures – just let your own and the children's creative ideas flow.

- Vary the technique by having the children draw around their hands (with some children you will need to do this for them), then filling the hand shapes with blobs of paint applied with the fingers. This is a much more controlled activity and requires greater dexterity and hand–eye control than hand printing as it is usually done.

- When the children have developed greater dexterity, put a different colour on each finger in 'rainbow order' (red, orange, yellow, green, blue), then with fingers together draw the hand across the paper in an arc and/or in more elaborate swirls.

- Also try nose or chin printing – take our word for it, this works well and is great fun. Knees leave good imprints too, as do elbows!

- The same ideas can be used for foot printing – very messy but again great fun. The feel of paint squishing through your toes is a strange sensation and for some children not pleasant, so always have a bowl of soapy water close by for lifting children out of the paint straight into the water. Tip: Use big toes if the foot printing is too much!

Printing Plus

As long as paint will adhere to the surface of an object (and as long as the object remains undamaged and can be washed clean afterwards), you can print with almost anything. Experimentation is the key; otherwise use junk or throwaway items such as tubes, pieces of wood, matchboxes, crunched-up paper, and so on. Using any of these and a large palette tray containing paint forms the basis of fun printing. An opened-out newspaper makes an excellent printing surface on a table because the paper 'gives' a little – a hard surface is difficult to print from.

Vegetable printing works very well because of the 'patterns' inherent in their shape – though ethically you may want to use vegetables past their sell-by date. Broccoli is one good example, although potato printing is a good place to start. Cut the end off the potato with a knife, dip this flat surface into paint and press onto paper. This will give an oval shape which can be 'built on', either by using the same shape dipped into another colour of paint or by the child using a spoon to scoop out shapes from the potato, dipping the 'new' surface into the paint and pressing onto the previous shape (using spoons is very safe and easy for children). If a new 'pattern' is needed, just slice a layer from the potato and the child can begin again. Children can experiment with their shapes to create multi-layers of patterns or use them separately on the paper to create varied designs.

Try and Dye

Very young children may have difficulty with dyeing: we often start using these techniques with three-year-olds, although of course you may find that more capable younger children can cope perfectly well.

Cotton fabric takes up dyes better than most other kinds of material. Both hot water and cold water dyes are available (Dylon offer a good range), although obviously cold water dyes are safer if you are preparing the activity while children are nearby. Wear gloves to mix the dyes as the colours will stain the skin.

Once you have a selection of colours ready, show the children how to use the fabric in different ways (always use wetted fabric before dyeing so that the dye can be absorbed into the fibres more easily). Each child will need a piece of fabric about the size of a handkerchief; anything larger than 30cm square will be cumbersome for younger children to manipulate.

- Concertina strips of the material and either secure each end with paper clips or tie round with wool or string.

- Screw the cotton into loose balls, again secured with string or wool.

- If the material is wrapped with white or natural-coloured wool or cotton string this, obviously will become dyed too and can be re-used subsequently in other art activities.

Top Tips!

Because it can take up to an hour for cotton to take up the dye, save time by using a microwave. Place the fabric and dye in a microwave-proof dish (making sure the dye covers the fabric to prevent fabric from burning), cover with clingfilm, 'cook' for four minutes, then rinse well and dry. It is advisable to use a microwave dedicated to this kind of use, not one that will also be used to cook food.

IDEA 22

Texturing

Prepare for this by obtaining a range of brushes and scrapers. These do not have to be specially bought – old toothbrushes and combs, windscreen ice scrapers, scouring pads, etc. will work perfectly well. Also have sponges, screwed-up balls of wallpaper and different kinds of cloth for the children to experiment with.

- Introduce texture work simply by having children apply paint of varying consistency to sheets of paper using the implements mentioned above (and of course any others that you think will produce a pleasing effect: use your own creativity and be flexible in your thinking).

- Roller the paint out on a (washable!) flat surface. The children make textures in the paint using their brushes and other materials. Place paper gently over the top (of the paint, not the children) and roller gently with a clean roller, then carefully peel the paper off to see the textured effect. The result can usually be hung up to dry without changing the effect of the picture because the paint should be virtually dry – if it isn't, too much paint was used initially and the children can learn from this experience.

- A variation of the above technique is to roller paint out on a washable flat surface, place a piece of paper over the top, clean roller over the top of the paper and then make marks on the paper with brushes or other implements. Carefully peel the paper off to see the effect.

- Place torn-up bits of paper on to the paint that you have rolled out on the table. Then place a sheet of paper over it all, and clean roller over the top, as above. Lift the paper and the shapes will come out as silhouettes in the finished product.

Collage

This is a rewarding activity on many levels:

- It allows children the freedom to tear, cut, glue, build, balance and design as they want.

- It gives children the pleasure of choosing and deciding on colours, shapes and textures.

- It allows them the opportunities to handle unfamiliar materials such as wood shavings, string, seeds, straw, papers and plastic, as well as fabric and papers of different colours, types and textures.

- It gives children the experience of learning how to apply glue in appropriate quantities, depending on the materials or media used.

Collage usually requires a more robust paper as a base than computer paper or newsprint. Sugar paper, cereal packet card and packaging cardboard are ideal. The base paper does not always have to be rectangular or A4: bases cut as squares, circles, diamonds, triangles and ovals can 'spark off' or add both interest to a child's idea, and a new dimension to the finished piece.

Provide as great a variety of textures as possible: selections of fabrics that can be easily cut or torn by a child, sweet wrappers, cellophane, coloured foil, sequins and tinsel, feathers, sawdust, buttons, old magazines, postcards and photographs, grasses and leaves, pressed flowers, twigs, etc.

Chalk Work

Chalks are readily available from discount stores and educational suppliers: also look for giant chalk sticks, which children find great fun to use and which produce very pleasing results. Be aware that chalk work is messy and much dust will be produced. You might find it advisable to have the children wear aprons and masks. Also check to be sure that none of the children have allergies to dust or other respiratory problems.

- Introduce chalk work by using sheets of coloured sugar paper. Encourage the children to draw using the chalk sticks conventionally, but then make patterns by drawing the sticks flat across the surface; smudge with the fingers to blend the colours and create patterns.

- Use small sponges, paintbrushes, toothbrushes, etc. to create further effects.

- Dip dry cotton wool into chalk powder, then dab the cotton wool onto paper. Later try dabbing the cotton wool using stencils for a more controlled result. Try using damp or wet cotton wool or paper for different effects.

- Make strong lines of colour in stripes either adjacent to each other or separate, and use brushes and sponges to spread and blend colours to create abstract art. Swirl the stripes with sponges to vary the effect.

- Make patterned edges along lengths of stiff card. Place the stencil edge on a sheet of paper and make a line of chalk along it. Either use a toothbrush to flick the chalk line out across the paper, or a stencil brush or fingertip to 'brush' the chalk on to the paper to create different effects. Repeat by moving the stencil edge slightly clockwise to create a fan effect, or use different card stencils to create patterns.

 Top Tips! **Preserve the children's work by spraying with matt varnish or hairspray.**

IDEA
25

Patterning

You can extend children's exploration of printing work with rollers. Most suppliers of art and craft materials stock plain rubber rollers, although these can be expensive. Cheaper ones made from sponge are available from DIY stores, and give texture to any finished picture.

There are also a number of manufactured textured rollers available, which have the advantage that the patterns repeat and line up exactly when printed. However, it is not very difficult to create the same degree of precision with home-made textured rollers; older children should be quite capable of doing this with your guidance. There are two ways of making your own patterned rollers:

- Using cheap sponge rollers, add effects by cutting away some of the sponge, wrapping string or elastic bands around the roller and by using different types of paint rollers, e.g. emulsion and gloss rollers.

- Alternatively, use some textured wallpaper cut to size, wrapped and glued around cardboard tubes. Use dowelling, index fingers or a pencil for the central rod, holding the tube down to roll. Cover the roller by brush painting the tube then roller out onto prepared paper on a flat surface.

Quite striking effects can be produced with patterned rollers. Use different coloured paints for blending effects. Print on paper or on card to make book covers, and consider embellishing the printed patterns with wool or string to make lines, zigzags, etc.

'Repeating rollers' of this sort help children to understand how patterns 'come round again'. This is a precursor to the concept of cycles, which can then be applied in many ways; from clock faces to water cycles to the orbits of the planets around the sun.

IDEA 26

Sculpture Work Using Papier Mâché

Papier mâché (from the French meaning 'chewed paper', though let's not take this too literally!) is a cheap and versatile material for sculpture work. There are many ways of making papier mâché, depending on the desired result: the following example is quick and easy for little ones to use.

Children can help with the process. Tear your paper into pieces, depending on the ability of the children or the moulds to be covered. The pieces can be strips up to 10cm long, but probably no smaller than 2.5cm square. Put them in a bucket, cover with water and soak overnight.

Work the mixture, making sure any lumps are broken up, then strain as much water as possible out of the pulp before compressing small amounts between hands to force more water out. Do not squeeze too hard or the pulp will become difficult to work with. The papier mâché is now ready to use.

Once a quantity of papier mâché has been prepared, the children use diluted glue and the pulp together to sculpt around plastic bowls, balloons, balls, etc. Start by brushing the 'mould' with glue, otherwise the pulp will not stay in place, then attach the pulp, then glue, then more pulp, etc. Pieces of cardboard or thicker paper can be attached and covered with pulp to add texture. The dried

results can be painted or covered with tissue paper and other materials. A useful project is for the children to create puppet heads that can be used subsequently for storytelling and drama.

Newsprint is cheap and readily available, but most types of paper can be used; tissue paper is good for details or creasing, blotting paper and egg boxes are good to use for their obvious strength. PVA glue is probably the most versatile type of glue to use. By using it straight from the bottle, the finished piece will dry quickly and be tough. By diluting three parts PVA to one part water the surface will be perfect for painting but takes longer to dry.

Both making models and sculpting with papier mâché are messy activities, so make sure the children's clothes – and yours – are protected. Use plastic aprons. A vinyl-floored art area or art room is ideal.

Bead Making

A huge variety of beads is available to buy these days. Some of them are very unusual and beautiful. But children can also make their own. Start simple and work up . . .

● Have the children cut plastic straws into either standard short lengths or different lengths (you may of course need to help some children with this), and use straws of various colours. The children then thread their 'beads' on to string, wool or ribbon to make necklaces, bracelets, etc. Roll sticky tape around the end of the string or wool to make the threading of the beads easier. This simple activity helps to develop hand–eye coordination. You can also use the necklace-making to revisit patterns and number work – create a bead pattern of your own and have the children copy it.

● Extend the idea by starting with plain paper straws. Have the children paint or decorate these before cutting and threading. Coloured wools and threads can be glued to the straws to vary the effect. This is another potentially messy activity (though strangely the children seem not to mind this), so prepare your work area as explained elsewhere.

● More elaborate beads can be made out of sugar paper or fancy wrapping paper. Plain papers can be painted or crayoned and decorated as outlined above. The children cut their paper in the shape of long isosceles triangles, then roll this shape starting at the wider end over a pencil or length of dowelling. Secure the pointed end with glue and then thread.

● Spherical beads can be made out of special modelling clay, which the children roll for themselves (different sized beads are fine). The centre hole needs to be added with a skewer before the bead dries. Embellish the beads by pressing smaller bought beads, glitter, threads, etc. into the dough when the beads are skewered, before removing and allowing to dry.

IDEA
28

Junk Modelling

Junk modelling is a cheap and varied activity. Impress on the children that in this case the 'junk' has both play and educational value. The principle of potential applies here. This informs us that creative thinkers can and do see potential for new ideas and projects in the most mundane of things. It is an important aspect of the children's creative development.

- At its simplest, junk modelling does not require glue or other adhesives. Encourage the children to build box towers and pyramids – how tall can they be made without falling down? Use boxes as 'bricks' to create pretend houses, caves, tunnels, castles, etc. Bigger boxes make brilliant playthings without doing anything to them, although they can be easily decorated and modified into vehicles of many kinds. Holes cut into large boxes can create buildings and can be used in imaginative play activities or to enhance rhymes and songs.

- If you or the children want to stick boxes together, consider sticky tape as well as just glue, as it is less messy and doesn't need to dry, thereby creating quick results which can be used straightaway. Help children to cut card circles to make wheels that can then be fixed to box cars, buses, trains and trucks using split pins.

- Use boxes, packets, jars and cans to create pretend shops. Children will play with these anyway, but you can enhance the activity by introducing toy cash registers and plastic money. This activity can be linked with number and money work and form part of children's social development as they rehearse the roles of customer, shop worker, etc.

Top Tips! Ring-pull cans are quite safe, but if you think edges are too sharp then line the inside edges with PVA glue, which forms a smooth protective surface when dry.

Tubes

Collect cardboard tubes of various lengths and diameters to use in the following ways.

- Skittles. Help the children to cut tubes down to a standard size. Decorate with colourful paper and/or add pictures and numbers. Use soft sponge balls or table tennis balls to play a simple game of skittles. Use the game to develop children's mathematical skills: How many skittles have been knocked down? How many are left standing? If the skittles are numbered the maths can be more demanding: Add up the numbers on the skittles that have been knocked down. What do they total?

- To increase coordination skills, spread out the skittles and ask the children if they can knock over the skittle with a specific numeral or picture on it. Using coloured skittles ask the children to knock over the blue ones first, then red, etc. Try using another longer tube to roll a marble down to help direction and aim (similar to the roll bar mechanism at a bowling alley).

- Candles. Decorate the tubes, stuff the inside with crêpe or tissue paper and have the children cut out red/yellow paper shapes to make the flames to stick on top of the filling or at the back of the tube.

- Tube People. Use a single tube for each person. Decorate with tissue paper, sticky paper, etc., or paint the tube 'body'. Draw a face and hands, cut these out and stick on. Elaborate on this simple design by painting the top and bottom halves of the tube different colours to suggest trousers/skirt/dungarees and top. Draw a vertical line down the bottom half to suggest two legs. Decorate further by adding buttons, ribbons, wool or cotton wool for hair.

More Tubes

- Tube Trees. Make palm trees with a painted central tube and fronds made from green sugar paper or card. Deciduous trees are made by pushing holes in the tube 'trunk' with a pencil and using painted straws for branches. Make leaves from sugar paper or card.

- Russian Dolls. Assemble several tubes of varying diameters. Make tube people as explained in Idea 29, but such that the tubes can be nested one inside the other.

- Children love playing with stacking beakers, which can be easily made using tubes and stiff card cut to form the bases, using tubes of varying lengths and diameters.

- Have the children look through comics and magazines for pictures of animals, or use pre-drawn outlines on card instead. Colour outlines as necessary or cut pictures out and stick on to thin card. Decorate a tube to represent the body of the chosen animal – using paper or paints, fake fur, cotton wool, threads, wool, etc. Stick the back and front outlines of the animal to the ends of the tube to make a representational beast.

- Tube Snails. These are slightly more elaborate and require the cardboard inner rings from rolls of sticky tape. The shell templates can be brightly coloured by the children and then stuck on the tube body.

Formal Shapes

Artwork activities help to establish a safe and enjoyable environment for children's creative development, which also acts as a bridge into other areas of learning. Noticing colours, patterns and shapes can be a valuable precursor to the introduction of concepts in science, number and geometry.

So-called 'formal' or classical geometrical shapes such as the circle, square, rhombus, equilateral triangle, etc., can be used in creative artwork sessions to explore repeating patterns, gaps in patterns, tessellations (regular interlocking patterns) and symmetry (see Idea 9). Here are a few ideas to start you off.

- Using equilateral triangles make a long, slithery snake by joining the edges together, turning in many directions to make the snake curl and twist over the base sheet. Give your snake a head so it can see where to go!

- If using white paper shapes for your snake, then a coloured paper base may be appropriate so that each triangle can be seen clearly. The shapes can be crayoned or painted to make a colourful snake, or different patterns or dots drawn on each triangle to make a very individual looking creature.

- Use various sizes of squares to create a range of mosaic pictures. These can be abstract, where the child just sticks coloured squares randomly on paper, or each square can be placed deliberately to make a picture. Random placing works well with squares cut out from pages of colour magazines, catalogues or photographs – the beginnings of montage, a picture made of pictures.

Top Tips!

Packets of ready-cut gummed paper shapes can be bought in most hobby craft stores and from educational suppliers. Or, of course, you can make your own templates: but as each shape will need to be cut out, staple together several sheets of paper before you begin cutting – depending on the thickness of the paper you can cut out several of the same shape each time.

Snake Game

To play the game you will need pieces of coloured paper cut into equilateral triangles (gummed paper shapes may save on sticking time), a base sheet of paper or card, a hexagonal piece of card, a matchstick or similar and counters, buttons or small paper circles and a snake.

Using the equilateral triangles make a long, slithery snake as in Idea 31. Allow the children to add the shapes so that the snake curls and twists over the base sheet: give the snake a head as this is the starting point of the game.

Stick coloured triangles at random on the base paper or place in specific repeating patterns, e.g. 1 blue, 2 red, 1 blue, 2 red, etc. This is the beginning of simple sequencing and can be extended to using three, four or more colours depending on each child's ability or interest.

Make a spinner with the hexagonal piece of card (six equilateral triangles). Each segment or triangle is filled to match the colours on each child's snake. The children may need help deciding on the variety of colours to use. Push a hole through the centre of the hexagon for a matchstick to be secured and you are ready to play.

Place a counter at the snake's head and spin the dice. Whatever edge it stops at is the next colour or pattern you move your counter towards.

IDEA 33

Mirror Imaging

Make sure that the small mirrors you buy for this activity are absolutely safe for the children to use. There are excellent sticky-backed shiny papers available from craft or educational suppliers which when stuck on thick card make good mirrors. Aluminium foil varies in quality but can be stuck onto thick card using double-sided tape for a quick alternative.

Encourage the children to use the mirrors to see if they can create matching symmetrical shapes:

- Try simple drawn shapes and then pictures. Help the children to realize that sometimes the object's reflection matches, and sometimes it doesn't. Also, when matches occur the symmetry isn't always down the middle (vertical symmetry).

- Draw simple pictures or outlines of an object. By experimenting with the mirror make one, two, three, four or more reflections of the object. Such manipulation takes practice but children are invariably fascinated at the result.

- Place a mirror in the middle of the picture of a face. Notice that the 'new' face doesn't look the same as the original face. Use a digital camera to take pictures of the children's faces and have them repeat the experiment using their own images. The effect will be even more striking to them then.

 Top Tips! Some arts software packages will allow you and the children to manipulate images in many ways – crop, stitch, tile, flip. As the children's capabilities grow, encourage them to transfer their creativity in art on to the computer (building in development of early ICT skills too). Even 'playing' with imagery in these simple ways is creative, insofar as it leads to further insight and greater understanding through the structured and systematic nature of the tasks you present.

IDEA 34

Exploring with Dry Sand

Sand play is not only fun but has great learning value. Explore using both dry and wet sand. A sandpit is useful for small group activities, although sand trays can more easily lend themselves to solitary play. Sand in a tray can be dried more quickly and easily than in a pit. However, both are useful in a preschool setting.

- Fill a tray that has raised edges with dry sand and make patterns using fingers, a stick, a fork, etc. Help the children to notice how the patterns are not 'fixed' or stable, because the sand grains do not stick to each other.

- Develop sand play by hiding sequins or other small 'treasures' in the sand so that children will come across them as they play.

- Further encourage sand play by offering children small play figures such as animals, dinosaurs and people. This can then become a group activity which helps children's socialization skills.

- Study the properties of dry sand further by looking at a variety of sand-flowing toys: sand wheels, sieves, buckets and sand timers.

- Encourage the children to notice the textures of sand. Dry sand is gritty and warm and flows like a liquid. Let them trickle sand through their fingers and listen to it fall on different surfaces to hear the variety of sounds of the grains as they drop.

Exploring with Wet Sand

- Prepare wet sand activities by adding water carefully, so that the sand is stiff but not oozing. Help the children to notice how sand changes colour when water is added – it becomes colder and heavier and can be used for building. Show children how making patterns with sticks or fingers, etc. is harder because the sand is stiffer, but how the patterns are more stable.

- Show them that a cupful of wet sand is heavier than an equivalent cupful of dry sand.

- Look at dry sand grains under a magnifying glass, then compare with wet sand where the water makes the grains clump together. Work with the children to help them express their observations.

- Look at how wet sand can be moulded using buckets or shape-moulds to create 3D models. Try the same activity with dry sand and very wet sand and notice differences. These simple observations act as an introduction to the concept of solid and liquid and the way that materials can be altered and made to behave differently.

- Use trays of wet sand to have the children make patterns with a range of objects: sticks, brushes, toy vehicles, etc. Encourage them to do leaf pressings, or use shells, fossils, hand and foot prints – in fact anything that makes a pleasing impression. A mould can be made of these impressions by using plaster of Paris. Mix the plaster with water until it is sticky and tacky and then pour into the print. Leave to harden (about 20 minutes) and then you can lift the cast away from the sand and brush off any grains that are attached. You may need to make a paper collar to go around the impression to prevent movement when pouring in the plaster mix. The cast can then be painted or otherwise decorated.

Section 2:
Listening, Sounds and Music

IDEA 36

Practising Quietness

These activities are precursors to developing good listening skills – and for quietening the mind.

● 'Let's see if we can be absolutely quiet for five seconds, ten seconds, longer . . . ' After five seconds – say 'Five!' and jump up in the air and jiggle, etc.

● Once the children can sit quietly for ten seconds, ask them to listen out for any sounds they can hear of things that are not being quiet. Talk about whether the sounds repeat themselves, like a clock ticking, bird singing, tap dripping. Or are they 'one offs' like a sneeze, car door shutting or something dropped? Talk about how these sounds are in the background when we are talking, running, being noisy but we don't always hear them because we are not listening to them specifically.

IDEA 37

Listening Outdoors

Quiet listening indoors and outdoors is very different . . .

Initially, have the children sit quietly for five seconds as in the previous activity, to allow them to become familiar with 'the air': listening in an enclosed space is 'cosy', whereas outside, though exciting for most, may create apprehension in some children. Introduce the activity with reassurances that all the children are safe and the sounds are just sounds that happen every day. Once the children have remained quiet for five seconds, say 'Five!' and jump up and jiggle (as before). Try to extend the time of quietness to ten or fifteen seconds. This is not so easy to do as indoors, so consider whether the children will find it easier by shutting their eyes.

As you listen to the sounds outside, guide the children towards making distinctions between natural sounds like the wind blowing, leaves rustling, etc. and 'man-made' sounds such as aeroplanes, road traffic, roadworks and radios. Point out repeating sounds like birdsong, a twig tapping on a window, people talking or walking in the street, dogs barking, children playing, laughing, balls bouncing . . .

Have the children concentrate on nearby sounds then those far away. Ask how we can tell the distances of sounds. Encourage children to notice what they are imagining as they listen. Such noticing of one's own thoughts, called *metacognition*, is an essential skill in developing children's creativity and thinking abilities.

Listening Games

Play listening games where children listen for subtle and particular sounds. Choose music with clear contrasts in it and with changes in the different musical elements such as tempo (fast / slow), volume (loud / quiet), pitch (high / low) etc. *Liszt's Piano Concerto No. 1* for instance is a rich example: it switches pitch, tempo and dynamics within the first few seconds, and the weave of sounds continually changes throughout the piece. It is lovely to use as background in art activities too.

In terms of metacognition (mentioned in Idea 37), attentive listening of this kind encourages exploring submodalities, noticing nuances and details of (in this case) auditory input and 'auditory thoughts'.

Know your music before the activity starts, obviously, so that you are familiar with the changes and can guide the children's attention. Keep extracts short to ensure concentration and add interest in chosen pieces by moving to the music appropriately – float and glide to waltzes, etc. Play a piece of music through once, and then again with the children listening for something in particular – the pop in Strauss's *Champagne Polka* is a great one to try!

Top Tips!

Music influences mood. Deliberately selecting certain kinds or pieces of music when you want particular responses and behaviour from the children will over time create a mental link between the two. This deliberate linking of stimulus and desired reaction is called anchoring.

IDEA

39

Clapping Games

Simple clapping games help children to explore rhythm, pace and volume.

- Start by clapping. Then change something about the clap: make it faster or slower, louder or quieter, etc. Ask the children to copy you. Change the clap again and ask the children to copy. Then ask a child to change something about the clapping, getting the other children to join in and follow the changes of the 'lead' child. Give other children in the group the chance to change the clapping. This activity, with children taking the lead, may need to be adult guided for some time until the children are familiar with the idea; once the children are confident, extend it in the following ways.

- Choose a child to start clapping out the pattern of his name (for example Jonathan – *one*-two-three). This introduces the concept of shorter and quicker, longer and slower, heavier and lighter claps and is a precursor to the children learning about stressed and unstressed syllables, time and rhythm and poetical metre later on in their school career. Ask the child to change the pattern by making it faster, louder, etc. and then after a time have another child change the pattern of clapping according to *her* name, and so on.

IDEA 40

Sound Games

- Auditory Mirrors. The children work in pairs. The first child makes a sound for his or her partner to copy exactly (like a mirror), then tries two sounds combined, then three . . . Swap roles. How many different sounds can they remember in succession? Extend the activity by focusing on pitch, intensity, duration, etc.

- Partner Play. The first child says: 'I have a sound for you. It is a (makes a sound).' The second child acknowledges the sound, saying 'Thank you for your (copying the sound as accurately as possible).' Then the second child changes the sound first given slightly and says, 'I have another sound for you. It is louder, softer, sharper, longer, etc. (repeating sound).' The first child thanks his partner by saying 'Thank you for your (making the sound).' Then the roles are reversed.

- Body Sounds. At first you can lead this, but later children in pairs or groups can think of examples for themselves: hands clapping, finger tapping, finger snapping, feet stamping, feet pattering, tongue clicking, lips smacking, lips kissing, whistling, blowing, bottoms thudding-sitting-down, etc.

- The children tap other parts of themselves. Instead of just clapping hands together, clap hands to knees, hands to thighs, fingers to thighs. Gently clap hands to cheeks, first with mouth open (not yours necessarily) then with mouth closed. Ask the children to notice the difference in sounds. Tap the body with just two fingers, then four. Do foot tapping. Have the children sit on seats in a circle and tap in rhythm just with toes, then balls of the feet, then heels, then with all of the feet. Which part of the foot is noisiest?

- Develop the game by having, say, every third or fourth child joining in using a different part of the body. This is similar to using four different instruments, but here their bodies are the instruments. This encourages teamwork and attentive listening.

IDEA

41

Listening with Eyes Closed

Every good preschool or classroom will have a selection of musical instruments. If you want to build up a collection we would recommend that you begin with maracas (which every child can play), woodblocks (including guiros and claves), tambourines in a range of sizes, triangles and whistles (plastic or metal rather than wood for reasons of hygiene, and always have wipes ready to clean the whistles during and after use). These instruments are all easy to use, robust and relatively cheap. Here are some ideas for developing the children's awareness and appreciation of sound.

- Take two instruments that make very different sounds: a triangle and a tambour for instance. Begin to attune the children's musical ear with these. Have the children notice and talk about how the sounds differ.

- Use one instrument and 'play' it so that it makes a range of sounds. Notice and talk about the differences. (Here we are exploring submodalities. See Idea 38.)

- Build up the number of instruments for children to compare and talk about. Draw out descriptive language from the children and use your judgement to introduce more words as part of their growing vocabulary of sounds.

- Use three of the same instrument – three maracas for instance – and help the children to explain how the sounds they make are similar, but different too, and sometimes in subtle ways.

- Progressively increase the range of instruments in your stock and therefore the variety of sounds that the children will experience. Try to include more unusual instruments for the children to use – finger cymbals, rain sticks, etc.

Sleeping Lions

Children pretend they are lions sleeping on the jungle floor, keeping as still and as quiet as possible to prevent capture. Initially the practitioner is the lion hunter, using a mixture of voice and simple drum rhythm to entice the children to move or wake.

The hunter prowls around the lions trying to wake them. If a child is seen to move, the hunter calls the child's name and takes them (the captured lion) to another area which is the 'pen'. As the captured lion enters the pen, the lions inside roar and jump up and down to entice the sleeping lions to wake up and join them. If no one moves the hunter might ask the captured lions to roar more loudly two or three times.

The hunter prowls around again and again until no lions are left sleeping. Once the lions are all captured, the hunter releases them back into the jungle so they can run, jump and leap around to a shaking of tambourine or maracas. Once the children are familiar with the game, the hunter can be a child and the instruments played by other children in the group.

Voices

- Record individual children talking. Play back the sound clips and have the group work out whose voice they can hear. Then ask the child whose voice is recorded to speak 'live' so that any differences can be noticed.

- Develop the simple voice-recognition game above by matching voice tone with moods. How do we recognize an angry voice for example? What is it about someone's voice that tells us they are happy or excited or nervous?

- Without using words, use your voice to make sounds that are happy, sad, angry, frightened.

- Make a link between voice tone, facial expression and body posture. Make happy sounds with a happy face and happy movements. Then try to make happy sounds without facial expression and posture.

And More Voices

- Partner work. Pretend you are from another country, world or planet. Imagine how you would communicate. Would you speak, use sign language, actions and body posture? Try all of these ways.

- Use action rhymes in a variety of voices. An easy one to learn and add to is 'Hands up high, hands down low / Touch your head, touch your toe / Say goodbye, say hello. Now let's do this one more time in a . . . voice.' Use a deep or giggly, shouting or whispering, foreign or nonsense voice – endless possibilities. You can even alter 'say' to wave, shout, laugh, etc.

- Deliberately mismatch voice tone and mood. Say 'I'm very very happy' in an angry-sounding voice. Why is that strange? Have the children say 'nice' words very loudly to hear how that changes the effect. Get the children to say 'You are my friend' in lots of different ways to raise their awareness of how the tone of voice at least as much as the words themselves expresses any emotion.

- Look at facial expression in connection with words and the tonal qualities of words. How do happy words sound? What does a happy face look like? Say 'I'm just a little bit happy' and have the children make facial expressions to show that mood. Then say 'I'm a bit happier . . . Now I'm a lot happier . . . Now I'm very very happy!' and ask the children to mimic that mood facially.

Top Tips!

Simple games such as these help children to develop their linguistic and interpersonal intelligences. Linguistic intelligence is the potential we all have to understand information conveyed through language (including voice tone, etc.). Interpersonal intelligence is the ability we possess to understand the relationship between people's thoughts (expressed through language), feelings and behaviour, and to communicate effectively based on that understanding.

IDEA 45

The Vocabulary of Sound

All of us take in information about the world through all of our senses. When we think about our experiences and what we understand, and when we use our imaginations, many people rely more on one sense than the others. In other words some people think very visually, while others imagine voices and are more attuned to imagined sounds. Another way of learning and understanding is *kinaesthetic*, where we have more physical tactile imaginings and are more in touch with feelings and body sensations. Some people will use two or more of these styles equally.

Helping children to develop all of their senses and thus to think more flexibly is important. In the context of recognizing and exploring how sounds can be changed we can explore the submodalities (constituent features) of sound in more detail.

Sounds are made up in this way:

- Volume (dynamics) – loud / quiet / soft.
- Tone – bass / treble.
- Pitch (timbre – quality and texture) – high / low.
- Tempo – fast / slow.
- Distance – close / far.
- Rhythm (the pattern of sound) – made up of long / short notes, silences and pauses – pulse and beat of music.
- Location.

Reprise

- Look back at the activities that we have already explored and think about how they might be developed or changed using other sounds or more submodalities of sound. Bear these in mind with the activities in the rest of this section.

- Sing a song with the children that they already know. Now sing it exaggeratedly slow and gradually speed up. Develop this by clapping or walking slowly initially to the song and as tempo increases, clap and move gradually faster.

- Ask the children to sit still and simply listen. After a while ask them to listen out for nearby sounds, then faraway sounds. Have the children make sounds as though they were very far away.

- Lullabies give children the opportunity to sing quietly, whereas marches allow them to sing loudly or with gusto. This develops flexibility in controlling volume, an important aspect of vocal communication.

- Sing songs about elephants/giants using deep, gruff voice sounds, or mice and bird songs in high-pitched squeaky sounds, to emphasize differences in pitch.

- Have the children sit in a circle and close their eyes. Position yourself somewhere in the room and whisper or make a quiet musical sound. Ask the children to point to where the sound is coming from. Change position and repeat. Develop this by making a musical note while moving around the circle to emphasize the change of location of sound. The children follow the sound by pointing their finger in the direction of the moving sound (without opening their eyes).

IDEA 47

Sound Words (Onomatopoeia)

Onomatopoeic words are those that make the sounds they are trying to name or describe. Bang, crash, splash, tinkle and boom are common examples. Develop children's understanding of this concept in these ways.

- Match animal pictures with the sounds the animal makes. So a cat goes *meow* and a dog goes *woof*. With older children you can point out that we can also say that a dog barks. *Bark* is not so obviously onomatopoeic as *woof*, but if you say it repeatedly the onomatopoeic quality becomes clearer.

- Match sounds with musical instruments – the *toot-toot* of a whistle, the *bang bang* of a big drum, the *ratatat* of a smaller drum. Always seek to extend children's understanding of onomatopoeic words in these contexts.

- Emphasize onomatopoeia in story telling. If the book itself doesn't use such words, improvise and put them in for yourself.

- Make a sound and say to the children, 'If this sound had a colour, what would it be?' Or: 'If you could touch this sound, what would it feel like?'; 'If this sound was a feeling inside us, how would we feel?' This encourages synaesthesic thinking (see Idea 2).

Finding Sounds

- Listen to recorded music to hear specific instruments being played. Classical music such as piano, violin and horn concertos give children the opportunity to hear specific instruments being played without too much confusion of other instruments being played at the same time.

- Listen to many types of music regularly in short bursts and the children will begin to pinpoint specific instruments being played. Even if they are unfamiliar with the name of the instrument they will start to recognize whether it is a wind, string or percussion instrument. For example: Beatles, *I Should Have Known Better* – mouth organ / harmonica; Bruce Springsteen, *My Home Town* – tambourine; America, *You Can Do Magic* – tom-tom.

IDEA 49

Making Bottled Music

Even making very simple musical instruments combines creative development with musical awareness and concepts of technology and design. Here are some starter ideas.

- Collect lots of different bottles; large, small, ribbed, plain, with or without tops to scrape and tap – add rice, pasta, small pebbles, sand, etc. to rattle and shake. (NB: We feel strongly that children should learn that food is not to be wasted and that in some parts of the world people have very little food. We therefore only use foodstuffs that are out of date and should not be eaten.)

- Fill glass bottles with water to different levels and tap with sticks and other implements to compare sounds. Tap one bottle with several implements to hear how different sounds can be made with the same 'instrument'. This activity requires careful listening to notice the differences.

- Put water in lots of different containers – pots, jars, teapot, a saucepan. Put straws in the water and blow through the straws into the water, listening to the different sounds the bubbles make.

- Have the children blow across the open tops of the water-filled bottles and explore making different sounds. This is a simple and very effective activity that works best with glass bottles rather than plastic. But you must of course be very alert and explain to the children that they must be careful with the bottles. Sometimes parents may voice their concerns, so be prepared to confidently justify the activity educationally in terms of the children's creative musical development. Explain that 'bottle music' develops focused attention and careful listening.

Making Musical Instruments

- Using different lengths and strengths of rubber bands on different sizes of boxes, pluck the elastic with fingers or pull a ruler or stick across the strings.

- Fill large straws or tubes with sequins, rice, lentils, pasta, shells, etc. and cap the ends, then paint and decorate.

- Claves (rhythm sticks) can be made by using dowelling cut into lengths no smaller than 15cm. Paint and varnish these or colour with felt-tip pens and tap a pair together to make music. Or simply use two pencils or pens and tap together: wood and plastic give different sounds, and while this is obvious to us it may well be a true learning experience for the children.

- Guiros can be made very simply by sticking a piece of corrugated card to a wooden block or cardboard box and by using your fingernails or a stick to scrape across the card. Or use the top or bottom edges of a CD jewel case and a pencil to make a very effective guiro.

- Cover one side of a small cardboard box or wooden blocks or bricks with different types of sandpaper to make a pair of scrapers which you rub together to make sounds or use a piece of dowelling to scrape one block, similar to a guiro.

Songs for Move- ment and Memory

Songs that have actions aid memory. There is a difference between recalling and remembering. Recall means 'calling ideas back again' from long-term memory into immediate conscious awareness: to remember is to re-member, to bring back into the members (the limbs and body) the movements, sensations and emotions linked with the ideas. To remember is always a more powerful experience than simply to recall.

- A well-known rhyme like 'Heads, Shoulders, Knees and Toes' is an ideal example of an action song. Sing it through a number of times with the children and show them the associated actions. When they are familiar with it, modify it in various ways.

- Miss out certain words but have the children touch that part of their body – 'Heads, shoulders . . . and toes.' This is a simple example of how the children will re-member that word.

- Change the parts of the body featured in the song. For example, sing 'Arms and elbows, knees and toes,' or fingers and thumbs, cheeks and chin, bottoms and backs, etc. Having the replacement body parts (as it were) associated and keeping the words alliterative also aids memory.

- Another song that children love is 'One Finger One Thumb Keep Moving'. This song is cumulative and its progression to longer and longer repeated lists helps children to rehearse the naming of the body in an enjoyable way, and also develops in them an appreciation of how the body moves.

- If you use the story rhyme 'Tommy Thumb' you or the children can draw faces on their fingers first. Each digit becomes a character who takes part in a song whose theme is meeting together, friendliness and teamwork.

My Own Rhyme

Always be prepared to improvise, change and play with rhymes and songs. This not only makes them fresher and more enjoyable for the children, but also you are modelling the very attitude and ethos of creativity that you want to develop in them.

With a rhyme such as 'Sally Go Round the Sun', change Sally's name for that of another child in the group. This makes most children feel very special – a song especially for them. Other rhymes where this works well are:

● 'Jack and Jill Went Up the Hill'

● 'There Was an Old Man Called Michael Finnegan'

● 'Polly Put the Kettle On'

● 'I Have A Little Brother, His Name Is Tiny Tim' (children are delighted to hear their name pop up in the *middle* of the song)

And there are plenty more. An internet search will often supply the words if you don't have them to hand, plus treasure troves of songs and rhymes that are less well known.

Top Tips!

Try having a nursery rhyme session just before the children go off to play, wash hands before meals, etc. Using a rhyme like 'I Went to the Animal Fair' gives the opportunity to put in several of the children's names and they will be the ones, for example, to go to the bathroom. Dismissing the children in staggered groups like this helps to avoid congestion and crowding.

Altered Rhymes

Nursery rhymes can be used in all sorts of situations, so memorize as large a repertoire as possible. It is perhaps stating the obvious to suggest that you should know all of the songs and rhymes by heart yourself. However, a 'prompt sheet' of song titles or first lines on hand nearby can be useful to give you confidence.

A rhyme wheel with pictures can be used daily at any time and is useful for filling moments between sessions or at the start of a group session, at the beginning of story time to introduce the story or at the end to complement the story just told. Such rhymes add to stories and there is usually at least one rhyme that can fit into any theme or topic – even more so if you change words within the rhyme, or deliberately muddle up beginnings, middles or endings of verses. This is good training for aural accuracy, and when the children spot the changes you can discuss the altered words and sense of rhyme.

Some examples:

> *Jack and Jill went down the hill, to fetch a loaf of bread*
>
> *Jill fell down on the way to town and Jack put her to bed.*

> *Diddle diddle dumpling, my son John*
>
> *Went to the beach with his wellies on*
>
> *One glove off and one glove on*
>
> *Diddle diddle dumpling my son John.*

Themed Songs

Using themed songs with the children is a precursor to the skills of categorizing and classification that they will develop later on. There is such a wealth of songs and rhymes (both traditional and contemporary) that you will rarely fail to find examples dealing with themes you want to emphasize.

As we have already said, feel free to make up new words to familiar songs when exploring themes like teddy bears, number, colour, etc. The children love doing this too, and most are very capable if they have the preschool practitioner's help. To help keep to your chosen theme, prepare a list of titles or first lines before your session to aid your memory. This also helps to prevent drying up or hesitating, and you can use it to give clues to the children about the next rhyme or song. The ideas and lists below are not exhaustive, and you will have your own favourites.

Popular themes include:

● Body parts: 'If You're Happy and You Know It'; 'Here We Go Looby Loo'; 'Knees Up Mother Brown.'

● Vehicles: 'I Had a Little Engine'; 'Down at the Station'; 'The Wheels on the Bus'; 'Aeroplanes, Aeroplanes All in a Row.'

● Animals: 'Daddy's Taking Us to the Zoo Tomorrow'; 'An Elephant Goes Like This and That'; 'If You Should Meet a Crocodile'; 'When All the Cows Were Sleeping.'

● Mice: 'I Think Mice Are Rather Nice'; 'Up the Tall White Candlestick'; 'A Windmill in Old Amsterdam'; 'Hickory Dickory Dock.'

Themed Songs using the Feelie Box

Use a feelie box (see Idea 71) in these ways.

● Put various items related to rhymes, e.g. a duck ('Five Little Ducks Went Swimming One Day'), a lamb ('Mary Had a Little Lamb') or a boat ('Row, Row, Row Your Boat'), etc. in the box. Have a child take an item out of the box and ask them to remember a song containing that item (making sure beforehand that the items feature in songs or rhymes the children actually know!). This helps develop memory as the children need to discuss their ideas and make connections, as well as focusing their attention with an element of mystery and surprise.

● Theme the items in the feelie box – all objects of the same colour, etc. This is more of a challenge to many children, who sometimes have to come up with a creative link to think of a song. So if a child pulls out an orange disc, button or counter the link might be 'The *Wheels* on the Bus Go *Round and Round*', '*Round and Round* the Garden like a Teddy Bear' or '*Oranges* and Lemons', etc. A blue cube could be 'A Jack-in-the-*box* Jumps Up like This', 'Little Boy *Blue*' or 'I'm a Little Robot, Short and *Square*', etc.

Tips for Using Music

- Always be familiar with any piece of music before you start any activity. This helps with your confidence in moving to the piece as well as being able to anticipate 'what comes next'.

- Keep extracts short to maintain children's interest. Time music you intend to use to be sure it fits with your planned activity and the children's attention/interest span.

- Use your own judgement as to whether a piece of music will suit the activity you have planned, rather than rely too heavily on what has been recommended. Try to arrange some 'personal listening time' to widen your experience of different composers, musicians, instruments and types of music. Compilations are a good source to dip in to when time is precious.

- Turn the widening of your own musical knowledge into an activity that includes the children. Fast forward or skip through pieces that you or the children dislike, although discuss why they or you are not enjoying a particular piece. This is as valuable as exploring why other music does appeal to you.

- Use mood music as an *auditory anchor*: that is, create a link in the children's minds between certain pieces and the moods that they evoke (and which you want the children to experience for whatever reason). Play that music whenever you want the children to enter that mood and frame of mind. Some symphonies and concertos are wonderful for quiet time: play them when children are coming in from boisterous activities outside, after physical exercise, etc. Rodrigo's *Concierto de Aranjuez* is a good example.

- Have a CD player available at all times. It can be a most powerful educational tool when you can call upon a wide range of music at any time and use it in a wide range of contexts during the children's preschool day or session.

Top Twenty-(one) Musical Favourites

This list is not exhaustive and is our personal choice. It is only a small selection of music that covers a wide range of tastes, and which we have found works well for listening, movement and rhythm activities with the children. Maybe you'll compile your own top twenty with the children's help . . .

- J. S. Bach – *Suite No. 3*

- Beethoven – *Moonlight Sonata*

- Brahms – *Hungarian Dance No. 5*

- Grieg – *Peer Gynt: Morning*

- Mozart – *Eine Kleine Nachtmusik*

- Scarlatti – *Keyboard Sonatas*

- Schubert – *Symphony No. 5*

- J. Strauss Jr – *Pizzicato Polka / Tritsch-tratsch Polka*

- Tchaikovsky – *The Nutcracker* ballet / *Danse des Mirlitons*

- Telemann – Concerto for Two Horns

- Sharon Shannon (a mixture of traditional country music from Ireland, Scotland, Portugal, Finland, Chile, New Orleans, etc: music for waltzes, jigs, reels, hornpipes, polkas. Instruments include fiddles, violins, accordions, bouzouki, bodhrans, harp, double bass, banjo, piano and other percussion instruments)

- Andean pipe music (traditional music from Peru, Bolivia, Ecuador, Argentina and Chile. Instruments include sikus (pan pipes), charango (ten strings similar to a mandolin), bombos (Andean drum) and guitars)

- Steel bands (music for calypso, reggae, soca, zouk, latin, conga)

- The Dancing Strings of Scotland (music for jigs, reels, strathspeys, waltzes)

- Beatles – *I Should Have Known Better* (mouth organ / harmonica)

- Bruce Springsteen – *My Home Town* (tambourine)

- America – *You Can Do Magic* (tom-tom)

- Sheryl Crow – *Fun* (guiro)

- Jim Gilstrap – *Swing Your Daddy* (backing vocals: 'Do wah dooby do wah' – Go on, try it out. You know you want to!)

- Mavericks – *Dance the Night Away / Think Of Me (when you're lonely)*

- Lipps Inc – *Funky Town*

IDEA 58

Rhymes and Movement Games

Act out familiar rhymes (or make up new ones) and turn them into a story. This incorporates story, rhyme, song, movement and active imagination. A few minutes' preparation is all that is needed and let your creativity flow! One starting point is 'We're going to visit a farm today':

- Seize the moment for pretend. Everybody looks out of the window. If it's raining sing 'Rain rain go away', or 'It's raining, it's pouring'. But we're going to the farm anyway: mime putting on wellies, coats, hats, etc. It might be muddy at the farm: sing 'Mud, mud, glorious mud'.

- Encourage the children to ask questions about their environment: their 'knowledge and understanding of the world' will develop all the more quickly when you cultivate curiosity. If there are puddles around sing 'Doctor Foster'. Think about how to get to the farm. Depending on whether you walk or go by bus or train sing 'Can you walk on tiptoe?', 'The wheels on the bus', 'Down at the station', etc.

- When you're on your way the sun comes out: sing 'The sun has got his hat on'.

- Once at the farm what animals can you see? Where are they? Are the chickens hiding? Look for them. Notice the ducks on the pond and horses in the stables. When Farmer MacDonald shows us his crops sing 'Oats and beans and barley oh'. Look at the scarecrows needed to keep the crows away: sing 'I'm a dingle dangle scarecrow'. Have a cup of tea and cake before leaving and sing 'I'm a little teapot', 'Polly put the kettle on' or 'Pat-a-cake'. However you get back to nursery, there are bound to be songs and rhymes to fit your return journey.

Other popular imaginary journeys are: going shopping; going on holiday; at the station; a trip to the zoo; a day at home; in the library; at the hairdressers; sitting in the garden; going to school; a bus trip.

Sound Lotto

Lotto games can be bought from educational suppliers or good toyshops, or with a bit of time you can make your own. The activity creates the opportunity for quieter children to take part as well as the more boisterous ones. All need to listen attentively and it is often the quieter children who 'spot' the sound first and encourage their noisier neighbour to look closely at their board.

Commerical sound lotto games consist of a tape, individual picture boards and coloured counters, usually for four or six children. There is also a set on the market with twelve cards of three pictures for a larger group. The pre-recorded cassette/CD is played and the tape stopped after each sound when there is a pause. If a child hears the sound of something that is pictured on their board, they put a counter on top of the picture. The round ends when the first child's board is full. However, you can continue until all the boards are full.

Another simple game for a whole group is to record sounds (with pauses between) that children are familiar with around the house, at preschool or out and about. During a listening session, play the tape and pause after each sound and ask the children to clap their hands, click their fingers or nod their heads (whatever your particular way of drawing attention might be) if they feel they know what could have made that sound. Ask a child what the sound is, where it might come from, what type of sound it was, etc. Children can be given stickers or counters when the sound is identified.

This activity can also be adapted to include pictures or photographs of the sounds recorded, to act as visual clues for younger children or where they may not be familiar with the type of sounds you have recorded.

IDEA
60

Musical Islands

This is similar to musical chairs, though without the music or the chairs! Instead there are rhyming words and mats (or strips of wallpaper – anything for the children to sit on).

All the children start by sitting on a mat or strip of wallpaper. Pretend these are the rocks or islands surrounded by water. Choose a pair of rhyming words such as jump/bump. Suddenly you shout 'Jump!' and the children jump off the rocks and islands into the water for a swim. While they are swimming, remove one or two of the mats. Then when you shout 'Bump!' the children have to swim to an island or rock which now is shared with a friend or two. Continue until there are a few overcrowded rocks and no more room can be found, then shout 'Swim for it!', and all the children jump into the sea and lie as still as can be on the floor. The first child to lie still chooses the two rhyming words for the next game e.g. dive/alive, float/boat, blue/crew, etc., or perhaps words that follow a theme.

Rhythm

Who's got it? Everyone! We can all dance to the rhythm of the music – use pop music, classical, waltzes, soul, polkas, reggae, soul, bhangra, opera, folk, calypso, ballroom, jive or just play a favourite rhyme, song or chart topper! The preschool practitioner's spontaneity and willingness to do this is part of the professional attitude. Try these activities to highlight rhythm with the children:

- Hold hands in a group together: swing arms, sway to and fro, wave arms.
- With partner holding hands, rock backwards and forwards, and sway to and fro.
- Bounce on knees or bottoms.
- Twist and bend.
- Stretch and curl up.
- Walk, march or slide.
- Crawl and wriggle.
- Use slow, strong movements – stepping, pulling, pushing.
- Use slow, light movements – floating, gliding, whirling, spreading, sliding.
- Use quick, light movements – flicking, darting.
- Use quick, strong movements – punching, stamping, whipping actions.
- Use scarves, ties, ribbons, veils or any strip of fabric to add to your dancing – flow or float.
- Use hats to add jerky or smooth movements to your dancing.
- Try it in wellies.
- What about hoops or quoits?

Circle Games

- Pass the Sound. This is similar to Pass the Parcel – children sit in a circle with one child in the middle. This child chooses someone to make a sound (either vocally or with an instrument), which is then 'passed on' clockwise, with each child repeating the sound, vocally or with the instrument, until the child in the middle claps his or her hands. The next child then changes the sound. The game can carry on until everyone has had a chance to change the sound or until a certain time has elapsed.

- Pass the soft toy. Use instruments and a soft toy with the children sitting in a circle. One child plays an instrument while the rest pass the toy clockwise and chant 'Pass the soft toy round / Pass the soft toy round / If the soft toy stops at you /You can change the sound.' At the end of the rhyme, the child holding the toy chooses an instrument and the game begins again.

- Variations on the 'pass the soft toy' rhyme can be made by changing the last line to say 'choose a (tapping, clapping, clicking, etc.) sound'; or swap the soft toy for an instrument which each child plays as it goes round, e.g. 'Pass maracas round / Pass maracas round / If a maraca stops at you /You can change the sound.' The child left holding the toy or instrument then decides on the new sound or instrument.

Ring Games

Most preschoolers are familiar with ring games like 'Farmer's in his Den' and 'Ring-a-ring-o-roses', and a lot of fun can be had with both.

Another favourite is 'I am the Music Man', which can involve walking and marching around to the rhyme while doing the actions and noises connected with each instrument chosen to play. A music man (either boy or girl) is chosen to stand in the middle of a circle of children who sing and clap along with the song. Once the music man has been asked what can be played, everyone joins in, copying the music man's actions, who then chooses another 'man' to stand centre stage.

'Look Who Comes Here Punchinello' is similar, and involves movement and actions, except this time 'Punchinello' is skipping, dancing, etc. around the outside of the circle of children, and when asked what he or she can do, Punchinello comes into the circle and 'performs'. The other children copy the action while everyone sings the song.

Simon Says

This is a very simple activity and ideal for young children. Arrange the children in a circle or in lines so that the adult can be clearly seen. Use simple movements: swaying, stepping forward and back, stamping and jumping, etc. Say 'Simon says jump like this/sway like this,' and so on for the children to copy. Then join up movements and make movements more complex or subtle to increase the challenge. Add music with a specific rhythm to 'dance' to.

The variations are endless. Let the activity be child-led with them choosing the two, three or four moves for everyone else to copy: again add music as appropriate. This can lead on to line dancing where the children can just step and clap together. Use country music (see Idea 57 or of course use your own favourites). Step from side to side, starting by stepping onto your right foot and closing with your left and vice versa. When you feel confident, clap your hands as you close your feet.

Line dancing with hands on hips helps with balance when you start to heel–toe. Stand on one foot and with your other foot, tap your heel and then your toe on the floor in front of you. The children copy and then try the other foot.

Use items from your dressing-up box: wear hats (particularly cowboy ones), scarves (as kerchiefs around the neck) and waistcoats to add to the effect. Try jumping and clapping, bending knees, sliding feet along the floor and wiggling hips, etc. There are many other steps that can be included depending on the age and ability of the children – improvise and invent. Your creative attitude is an excellent model for the children's own behaviour.

Musical Stops

Musical stops can take various forms:

● Initially use a song like 'Half a pound of tuppenny rice'. Talk about the length of the body of a weasel, slim and slinky. As everyone sings along, move around the room or floor 'like a weasel' to the music. Towards the end of the song, instead of singing 'pop' goes the weasel everyone shouts 'STOP goes the weasel'. Everyone stops and either sits down as quickly as they can, or makes a statue. This gives the children plenty of warning, as the rhyme is very familiar and they know exactly when the stop is coming. You can continue until the children are fed up (this might be a long time!).

● An obvious follow-up is to use any rhyme or song with a 'wow factor'. Clap hands or use an instrument with a specific beat (e.g. a drum, cymbal or whistle) at the appropriate point. Children can take turns to be the 'stopper' or 'statue maker'.

● Encourage the children to make statues that follow the rhyme; for example, in 'Hickory Dickory Dock – clock struck ONE', stand as straight and tall as possible like a numeral one, or curl up small like a little mouse.

● When music is added, first allow the children to see when the pause or stop button is pressed. This gives them time to prepare to change from moving around to actually stopping. Begin the game like this because children might not be attuned to the subtleties of many instruments playing together.

IDEA 66

Musical Hats

This is a similar activity to musical chairs, but without the need to move around.

- With all the children sitting in a circle facing each other's backs (i.e. sitting behind each other), place a hat, handkerchief or a square of fabric or crêpe paper on each head. When the music starts, each child takes the 'hat' from the child in front of them and places it on their own head. This continues until the music stops. Each time the music stops one hat is removed from a head. The music then starts again but the next time the music stops, the child without a hat has to sit out of the game. The game continues until only one hat and two children remain: they sit facing each other and continue to remove and replace the hat until the music stops and the child with the hat on can take a bow.

- The musical activities as previously described can be extended to include the use of hats, scarves, gloves, etc. When the music stops swap the items of clothing from the dressing-up box: this means that no one 'wins'. Everyone can take part until the end of the song, or when the time is up, or the children become disinterested.

- Alternatively, when the sounds stop or the adult claps, move in a different direction, touch toes, twirl round, etc.

- Play musical stops with a partner and when the music stops hold hands or touch each other's knees, etc. Let the children add their own ideas.

IDEA 67

Marching Band

Any sort of marching type music will enhance this activity, for instance: military bands; brass bands; Berlioz – *Rakoczy March*; Elgar – *Pomp and Circumstance March*; J. Strauss Jr – *Radetzky March*.

First sit the children comfortably and give time for them to listen to the music. You will probably find that several children begin making spontaneous movements, tapping or even humming along once they hear the rhythm of the music. When you feel ready, start clapping with your hands or tapping your feet, then begin to move around the room. You will find that many children will join you and begin marching – the music suggests that type of movement. Some children may prefer to stay sitting and clapping until they feel comfortable about joining in.

Develop the activity in further sessions:

● Try using the same music – children love repetition. Talk about bands and how they march in lines. Have the children try it for themselves: show them how to swing arms along as you march in time.

● Give the children instruments they can tap or strike as they march.

● Try stamping/stomping/striding/jogging to see which works best with the music.

● March in time to the music – double time, half speed, freeze games.

● Enrich the session by making simple peaked caps. These are easy to create and can be decorated in the band's colours and worn on the next march.

● Try different types of music – does marching to it work?

● Clap and move to waltzes, polkas, etc. (this is also a good way of introducing children to classical music and multicultural songs).

Partners

Partnership games can greatly increase a child's confidence.

Organize groups of three children. They decide which two are going to be in the boat and who will be the crocodile swimming around in the water. The roles will be swapped for the next song, so no one will miss out. The two boatmen sit facing one another on the floor with legs side by side and touching each other. By reaching slightly the children hold hands and lean forwards and backwards, forwards and backwards, as though rowing the boat, while the third child, the crocodile, swims around the boat. Everyone sings, 'Row, row, row your boat, Gently down the stream, If you see a crocodile, Don't forget to scream!' The two children rowing scream and jump out of the boat and the song begins again with a different crocodile swimming around.

After the third time of singing the song you may find that the children come up with other sea creatures that they could sing the song about, such as sharks, whales, eels, etc. The children rarely tire of games like this – the adult usually gives in before the children!

Hand Jives

Although rock and roll music is excellent for doing hand jives, as long as there's rhythm, there can be hand jives, though we're not sure the results can be called 'jives' technically, but it's fun and enjoyment that we're going for here.

Make fists with your hands and tap one hand on top of the other once, twice or three times and swap over hands. Do this in time to the music.

When the movement and rhythm are established, with hands flat and horizontal and palms down, shake each hand over the other and then swap, once, twice or three times. Put the moves together and you have a hand dance.

Now put one fist under the elbow of the other arm which is held upright and with the index finger raised make a circular movement – once, twice or three times – then swap. Add this third move to the jive.

With index fingers outstretched and the rest closed over the palm, circle fingers around each other, one way then the other – once, twice or three times: this is the fourth move. Put them together and you have a more intricate hand jive.

Once the children are familiar with and feel capable of doing a couple of the hand movements you can challenge them by adding these others. And the possibilities go on – the children will have ideas of their own and often the 'jive' involves slapping thighs, rubbing tummies, shrugging shoulders, etc.

Remember that these activities are not frivolous or lacking in educational value. A simple hand jive develops children's coordination and enhances the ethos that we have been advocating throughout this book, which is that creativity and learning flourish in the presence of fun and play. We are also cultivating children's uninhibited enthusiasm to explore – in this case, how their bodies can match the rhythms of the music you have selected.

Recognizing Different Instruments

Choose two instruments, bought or home-made. Begin the activity by linking simple movements to match each sound, so that the children will remember these easily (e.g. drum – sit down, claves – stand up). You can have fun with this because the children will think every time they stand up they will then sit down and vice versa. So by repeating one of the sounds once or twice on occasions, or otherwise varying the pattern, the children will begin to realize that they do have to listen to be able to respond to each sound appropriately.

Progress to three instruments, adding a maraca perhaps at which, when shaken, you jiggle or wriggle; this might happen when the children are sitting down or standing up. As the children's confidence and ability increase, speed up the playing of the three instruments until the pace is too much and everyone is giggling.

More fun can be had by increasing to four instruments (include turning round to the sound of a guiro), and by enlisting the help of children to play the instruments. There are many variations of the basic activity: e.g. tap heads to a triangle, touch toes to a whistle being played and so on. Encourage the children to come up with some ideas too!

We have never tried changing the movement to a different instrument during the same session – but it may be worth a try!

Section 3:
Imagination, Words and Feelings

Feelie Box

Use a box or drawstring bag whose size will depend on the activity you want the children to do. What matters is that none of the children can see what's inside. The box must have a hole big enough to place a hand through. If another side can be opened, then larger items can be put inside to extend the activities.

Put different kinds of paper in the box. The sounds they make when scrunched up will be less obvious than those of musical instruments. Get the children to listen carefully and tell you if you are scrunching crêpe paper, tissue paper, cellophane, foil paper, newspaper, the inside of a biscuit tin or chocolate box, etc. Sandpaper can be scraped by a fingernail rather than scrunched. You can also have examples of such papers on card so that the children can point to their choice if they don't know the word for it. And of course let the children use the feelie box too so that they can develop their awareness of the relationship between the sound and feel of different materials.

Tip: Sometimes children will make up their own words to describe the sounds they can hear. Write these words down (helping the children to make them sound right if necessary) so that the children have a visual reference. Just as importantly, you are valuing the children's thinking and implicitly letting them know that even such made-up words are valid and useful.

Useful sound words include: loud; soft; smooth; clear; fuzzy; sharp; grating; crackly; scratchy; rasping; muffled; short; long; sad; bright; dull; tinkling; popping; slapping; slopping; whooshing; slushing; thudding; plodding; picking; rattling; jingling.

IDEA 72 Animal Sounds

- Use the feelie box/bag described in Idea 71. Obtain a collection of *realistic* plastic play animals. Have a child feel for one in the box and make the sound that animal would make for the other children to guess. Prepare for this activity by showing the children the animals as you put them in the box, and begin with two very different animals that the chosen child knows, so that the child doesn't fail. A good guiding principle is to try the activity by yourself first. If you can't feel the difference between a sheep and an elephant then most likely the children won't be able to either.

- Regularly use songs and rhymes that feature animal sounds, e.g. 'Old MacDonald Had A Farm', 'I Went To Visit A Farm One Day' or other rhymes where instead of singing the type of animal at the appropriate point, you make the noise for the children to guess which animal it might be.

- Encourage small-world play activities featuring animals. Small play farms and zoos are easily obtained and children love to play with them. Link their play with more systematic activities that explore sound.

- Add to the children's learning whenever you can, for instance by explaining that an animal will make different sounds for different reasons, to communicate affection, anger, distress, etc. Talk about their pets at home and suggest differences in how they ask for food, walks, play or to be let outside.

IDEA 73

Themed Story and Rhymes

Consolidate children's learning and understanding of themes by, for instance, following up a story with some rhymes and songs. If you read *Goldilocks and the Three Bears* with your group, do some rhymes or songs that emphasize the number three or bears. For example: 'When Goldilocks Went to the House of the Bears'; 'The Bear Went Over the Mountain'; 'I Know a Teddy Bear'; 'Three Blind Mice'; 'Three Little Kittens'.

These songs can be acted out and dramatized along with the initial story.

Here are some other ideas.

- After reading the story of *Elmer the Elephant*, recite poems or rhymes or sing songs about elephants ('An Elephant Goes Like This and That'; 'Nellie the Elephant') or colours ('Baa Baa Black Sheep'; 'I Can Sing a Rainbow'; 'Ten Green Bottles').

- Then add movement to the activity. Lay some string out on the floor and have the children pretend that they are elephants balancing along a wire while singing the song 'One little elephant balancing, step by step on a piece of string'. Although this rhyme ends when the fifth elephant joins in and the string snaps, this need not be the end, as you only need the string to snap when the whole group has 'balanced' or the string is too short for any more 'elephants' to join in. No one need be left out. This simple game develops both imaginative play and physical skills.

Rhyming Words

Play repeating sound-word games – pet, vet, set. It doesn't matter if 'nonsense' words are used (e.g. zet) – this is a further good opportunity for creative exploration.

- Make up rhyming words with names – Pally Sally, curly Shirley, handy Andy, jolly Molly.

- Make up rhyming phrases with names – Trendy Wendy's very bendy, Dan the Man how he ran, Jill is brill runs up the hill, etc.

- Make up nonsense rhymes with names – wicky Vicky, soary Rory, dayla Shayla, filmit Simrit.

- Make up simple rhyming chains – Sheep leap, cats sleep, eyes peep / Dogs bark, ink marks, cars park / Lambs skip, papers rip, crabs nip.

- Use colour words in rhymes – Mr White got a fright in the middle of the night / Mr Yellow likes to bellow, now he's mellow / Mrs Red went to bed, with a hat upon her head.

- Finish rhyming couplets: I'm thinking of a word that sounds like mouse, we live in one, so it's a (house); I'm thinking of a word that rhymes with tall, but it's just the opposite, so it is (small); I'm thinking of a word that sounds like shop, if it isn't the bottom, it must be the (top).

- Make a book of things that rhyme. At the top of each page write a chosen word then draw or stick pictures on the page along with words that rhyme.

- Make pairs of cards with pictures that rhyme – cat / hat, blue / shoe, hen / pen, house / mouse, tree / bee, etc. Play matching games like snap or Pelmanism with the cards, winning pairs that match rhymes. Use the same cards in threes to spot the difference. Add paper clips to the cards and play magnetic fishing for matching rhymes.

'I Spy' with a Difference

- Collect a group of pictures suggesting certain sounds, e.g. bird, door (with doorbell), cat, dog, frog, snake, lion, flag, vehicle, etc. Say 'I hear with my little ear something that makes this sound – flap, hiss, roar, miaow, tweet, purr, ding dong, etc.' Children guess the picture, and then perhaps could suggest other sounds that those 'pictures' might make.

- Using several instruments that make very different sounds, say 'I hear with my little ear something that sounds . . . '. The children then have to guess which instrument it is: 'jingly' could be a tambourine or handbells, so be aware of the instruments you choose and their sounds.

- Collect a group of objects or instruments and say 'I hear with my little ear something that sounds hollow, solid, metallic, made of wood, metal, has holes in it, etc.' Some may sound similar, so then describe the differences using 'sound' words – longer, quieter, deeper.

- Introduce or revisit alliteration by saying 'I hear with my little ear something that makes a big bass bang boom!' or 'a teeny tiny tinkly trill' or a 'whispery swishy hissy ssshhh'. Prepare for the activity by having at least one item (or a picture of it) that makes the sounds you are suggesting, in this case a drum, some little bells and cloth or curtains.

Random Choices

Many years ago the thinking expert Edward de Bono highlighted the value of randomness and chance in stimulating creative thought. Introducing a random factor encourages the generation of unexpected ideas. For these activities choices can be made at random but within a theme by using a quick and easy-to-make 'decider'.

- Make a hexagonal spinner (see Idea 32). On each segment draw or stick a picture, word or numeral: spin the wheel and use the chosen picture to suggest the song, rhyme or story.

- Alternatively, prepare something more elaborate: a 'decider wheel' is a very useful tool. It can be used in many ways, for story telling, singing, group activities, topics, etc., depending on the pictures or words put on the base wheel. To make it you need two circles of card (not less than 20cm diameter), a brad or split paper fastener and pictures, stickers or words. Mark the centre of each circle and divide the base wheel into segments (like an orange cut crossways). Put the pictures or words in each segment. A 'window' is cut out of the top card to show the picture or word on the base wheel underneath. The size of the window depends on the size of pictures or words on the base card. Put the pictures like a clock face so that as you turn the top wheel, the pictures are upright. Join the two wheels together with the split pin or brad. Your decider wheel is ready to use. Move the top wheel around and sing a rhyme or song or tell a story about the exposed picture or word.

- Try cutting a second window in the top wheel and using extra pictures, stickers, words or numbers added to the base wheel. Then as the top wheel is moved around, two items are shown. This demands more complex linking of ideas from the children.

IDEA 77

Spontaneity

Spontaneity is not effective without preparation! The children need to have developed their listening skills to be able to respond meaningfully through mime, movement, etc. as music plays, using the music as a guide to movement. The creative agenda of this and similar activities is *spontaneous interpretation*, so it helps when you and the children are familiar with the music.

Some children are naturals at movement, mime and dancing, and feel at ease with this kind of activity. Others are more tentative and your choice of music or song needs to be carefully considered so as to be inspiring to all the children. And of course your own enthusiasm will rub off on them. Children mimic adult role models, so if you seem lethargic or uninterested in a particular piece of music, the children will respond to your mood likewise.

Encourage the children to 'feel' the music. Some children prefer to assimilate the music through the floor (vibrations and warmth), others with eyes closed tightly, some sitting upright, others curled up. Be flexible and allow the freedom for children to listen to the music in their way, as long as they are not disturbing others around them. Even very young children are developing or have established preferred learning styles.

Some children will be ready to move before others: if you have the space available allow them to do that. However, if your space is limited then you may have to restrict the length of listening time. This is something you will need to judge. Then play the music again and let their imagination roam.

Group Mime

Link and formalize music and mime: using suitable music or voice sounds, have the children role play being trees, birds, rivers, vehicles . . .

- Have a group of children pretend to be birds: swooping around the room, flapping their arms – whatever they feel is appropriate to being a bird, or flock of birds. See if the other children can guess what they are. Add sounds and let everyone join in.

- When the children are comfortable doing the mimes in a group, they may feel confident enough to mime individually. Have a selection of cards with pictures of objects or animals that can be 'copied', either in mime or voice, or both. Place them face down and allow the children to pick a card to mime, or help them to 'make up' their own.

- Your next step might be to mime a nursery rhyme without singing it, and have the children guess which rhyme it might be. This may need to be adult led but eventually the children will be able to take over.

Group Role-play

Children love play-acting, whether it's in the home corner, on the bikes outside, in the water play tray . . . Children live in a world of pretend as they rehearse the roles, rituals and relationships of the real world. It is their way of preparing to fit in. While engaging in this kind of make-believe they organize themselves and often each other in their play: it comes naturally.

Organizing role-play for a group is best if the children are familiar with the situation, so using a rhyme such as 'The wheels on the bus' is a good start. Put chairs out, appoint a conductor and driver, sing, add your own verses and act out.

IDEA

80

Dressing Up

Most young children like to dress up and be someone else as they act out a role. Interestingly, such fantasizing allows some children more freedom to express themselves, so dressing up can be an excellent way of encouraging a shy child to blossom.

Your dressing-up box or cupboard should reflect a wide variety of clothing from many cultures. Children can be given factual information about the clothes and by whom, where and why particular costumes are worn. Take the opportunity (using visuals as necessary) to discuss how both men and women throughout the world wear trouser-like and skirt-like clothes.

Dressing up can be considered under three categories:

- Everyday clothes, including formal uniforms.
- Special occasion clothes, including parties, weddings, etc.
- Fantasy clothes, including superheroes or simply mismatched clothes or bright colours.

Ensure that the range of clothes is suitable for boys as well as girls: include trousers as well as dresses, men's shoes and women's footwear, etc.

No Need for Costumes

Sometimes ideas for role-play or dressing up come from something as simple and as easy as adapting a paper bag, a piece of card and string or a length of fabric, by adding a few 'crafty' bits to aid the illusion.

- Paper bags can be used to make masks or different heads, with holes for eyes and 'eyebrows' made of fur fabric or wool. Pinch corners of bags and tie with ribbon or thread to make ears or 'pony tails'.

- Pieces of card can be cut to different shapes to make simple masks, with eye slots or holes to peep through. Decorate with glitter and sequins for a fancy dress ball, or with feathers and paint to be an owl or parrot. A round sponge (from pill bottles) can be stuck on for a pig's nose.

- Rectangles of fabric tied around the neck with the other two ends around wrists make capes or 'wings' to create a bird or superhero.

- Put a strip of card around the forehead, coloured or decorated and with feathers added to make an Indian chief or squaw.

- A wide strip of card around the forehead, decorated with glitter, foil, etc. creates a prince, princess, king or queen.

IDEA

82

Props

Imaginative play activities need not involve specific play corners or expensive equipment to be successful. Charity shops, jumble sales and car boot sales are good sources of props (and toys, books and other useful material). And of course because the emphasis is on developing the children's imagination, sticks, boxes, pieces of cloth and other simple items are often more useful and enjoyable than elaborate or realistic toys.

A wide selection of items can transform a child in many ways, from being 'only themselves' to any number of magical characters. Dressing up enriches the make-believe worlds of every child – but always have a full-length mirror to hand as well. Children love admiring their outfits and how they look in them. Our recommendations for basic props are:

● Pairs of spectacles (with lenses removed, unless they are plastic): a special agent, able to see around corners, a simple disguise.

● Handbags, baskets, shopping bags, briefcases, purses: aid a shopping trip.

● Plastic red noses and bow tie: a clown.

● Hats and caps: wedding party, old lady or man, football fan, police – attach two plaits made from old tights and tied with ribbon to a hat for long hair.

● Gloves and mittens: decorated with fur fabric to make a monster.

● Ties and belts/wigs/masks/shoes, slippers, boots/jewellery (safely strung)/scarves and lengths of fabric or ribbon.

Play Corners

As imaginative play activities are essentially social, play corners give children the opportunity to understand the views and needs of others. They are an ideal way for children to explore roles taken from the world of adults and act out behaviour that would not be possible in their everyday lives. Children can learn about other people and relationships, as well as recreate experiences in their own lives.

When we first started working with children (over 30 years ago), Wendy houses were usually the only kind of play corner to be seen, perhaps changing into a shop if that related to the topic of the time. Nowadays, play corners have been developed to include almost any scenario a child might come across, from a home corner or café, to a hospital or veterinary surgery, a garage or an airport, a jungle or a circus. There is so much imaginative play equipment available that almost any idea can grow! However, sometimes there can be a tendency to overplay ideas; often the simplest pieces of equipment will have the richest play value and serve the purposes you are aiming for.

Some ideas for play corners have to be thought about carefully. There are hygiene and safety issues with a doctor/dentist surgery that features spatulas, thermometers, long-handled mirrors and so on. It might be prudent in such cases to put limits on how realistic the children's play should be – though do exploit the opportunity to talk with them about hygiene and cleanliness.

Developing Play Corners

Some of the most successful play corners in our experience focus on a picnic with or without teddy bears, a tea party, birthday party, campsite, veterinary surgery, post office, library, circus clowns, garage, hairdressers or shop (toy, grocer, shoe, book, etc.). Most of the equipment was already in and around the nursery or 'borrowed' from parents or staff.

There is no real need to spend a great deal of money on elaborate equipment. Drape fabric over chairs or tables to make caves, tents or dens. Use assorted cushions to make mountains or avalanches. Mats can be used as boats, magic carpets or desert islands.

Chairs arranged in rows can become cars, buses or trains so that the play 'corner' can be a role-play activity for a larger group. A pretend train, coach or aeroplane trip only requires a few props and, with a little adult involvement initially, the children can be left to explore their own imagined trip around the country or world. These ideas are swiftly and easily set up with a bit of forward planning. All that is needed is imagination and some floor space.

Tip: If you can visit the 'real play corner' beforehand with the children, even more experiences will come out of the play opportunities you provide.

TV Inspired

Television programmes can become the basis of rich, successful and varied play corner games. Children love the characters from their favourite TV episodes and take great delight in being a 'famous' person or animal.

- As *Bob the Builder,* a child can 'fix' anything, with lots of scope for additional 'friends' to join in. Use boxes, hard hats, telephones, walkie-talkies, etc. Extensions of this idea are to create a building site/DIY store/painters and decorators' business as a play corner.

- Recreate *Dora the Explorer* with made-up maps, compasses, magnifying lenses, boots, etc. Her 'pal' Boots can be a soft toy or another child. Extensions of this idea include the scenarios of a desert island or archaeological site, or thinking about road safety or camping.

- Children can become *Postman Pat* with parcels, letters, (toy) cat, and a van made of painted cardboard boxes. Extensions of this idea are to create a post office, sorting office or delivery services.

- *Fireman Sam* is an ideal way of starting a theme on the fire service.

- *Pingu* can be the basis for a topic on the Antarctic, conservation, and links to other stories where animals are treated as people.

- Colour topics could include the characters of *Barney, The Fimbles, The Tweenies* or *The Mr Men.*

Top Tips!

Spend a few hours watching children's TV and see what ideas you can come up with.

IDEA

86

Scarves

Simple squares of fabric make headscarves. Some basic activities (perhaps with music on in the background) for using scarves include:

● Initially encourage children just to 'play' with the scarf – flick it, shake it, etc. to get to 'feel' what it can do and what they can do with it.

● Use the scarves to wave to a friend – try to attract their attention with no voice, only movement. Say goodbye in 'scarf language'. Are the actions the same?

● All children stand in a circle and sing and do the actions to the 'Hokey Cokey' using their scarves.

The following activities are quick and involve lying on the floor with the scarf or square of fabric over the child's face.

● Have space around the children to allow them to move. Tell them to put the scarf over their face, 'Now move your fingers – have you shut your eyes? Wriggle your toes, feel the movement . . .'

● Gently blow the fabric and feel it move on your face. How hard do you have to blow to 'see' around you?

● Listen to the music. What is it saying? Is it easier to listen with something covering your eyes?

Alternatively, a Chinese-style 'dragon dance' can be enacted using scarves (see Idea 87). You will need a length of fabric that several children can 'hide' underneath, and that is wide enough for them to hold the edges.

Ribbon Dances

Ribbon dances work well with waltzes or similar music that has a gentle, floating, gliding quality. Prepare a wide and varied selection of lengths and widths of fabric or ribbon: younger children will need narrower and shorter lengths, to prevent tangles and subsequent frustration! 'Feel good fabrics' include chiffon, satin, silk and polyester. Provide plain colours and prints (both will inspire), and a variety of lengths, though initially not longer than the height of the children.

Rather than simply telling or showing the children how a ribbon dance works, listen to the music and draw the children's attention to the way it flows. Match this with swirls of a ribbon and the kind of movements you want them to copy.

Once the children are 'feeling' the music and perhaps swaying to it, let them choose their own ribbon, and explain to them how it's used as an extension of the child's arm, and that by moving rhythmically the ribbon will move: keep it moving and it won't tangle. Once they are confident and enjoying the experience have them try a longer length, or two ribbons. Subsequently discuss how difficult longer or wider pieces are to manipulate.

A more ambitious related activity is the Chinese-style 'dragon dance'. This can be enacted in a similar way with a length of fabric that is wide enough for several children to hide beneath and wide enough for them to hold the edges. With Chinese music playing the children can move, undulate and weave around the room. This is a memorable way to celebrate Chinese New Year.

Parachute Play

You will need one or more circular pieces of fabric. The circumference of the parachute will determine the number of children who can be involved, as they each need space to hold the edges of the fabric with both hands. Brightly coloured 'parachutes' can be obtained from educational suppliers, and are well worth the investment.

Parachute play requires space, but if using outdoors be prepared for breezes moving the fabric and perhaps pulling the edges from children's fingers: some children find this fun and exciting, but others are less confident and can become apprehensive. A smaller circle of fabric is fun for four or five children to play with on their own, as they discover how the fabric floats, billows, drifts and ripples.

The first time you use a parachute explain how exciting it will be, but that everyone has to work together. Begin with the children kneeling in a circle so that there is little opportunity for them to run underneath the fabric. Then with you in the middle of the circle, give out the edge to the children so that the parachute unfolds and is spread out without fuss.

Lay the parachute down and show the children your thumbs, which you then tuck under the fabric with the rest of your fingers on top. This is the 'parachute grip'.

Count to three and everyone stands up and throws their arms in the air, while still holding and *not letting go* of the parachute. The chute will rise and then slowly drift down. (Adults should take care not to lift their arms fully, as this will pull the fabric from children's hands.) Repeat several times.

Build up the length of the sessions over time, as the muscles in the children's arms and shoulders will tire very quickly. This will increase the children's stamina for further games.

Parachute Play Plus

Before starting a more prolonged parachute activity, do a few loosening-up exercises with the children: shaking hands and arms, shrugging shoulders and generally relaxing upper body muscles. Then start the activity as described in Idea 88, holding the chute in the parachute grip, and continue by:

● Kneeling down and shaking the chute to see the shapes that are made. Allow two or three children to experience the 'feeling' of running on the moving fabric.

● Play crossovers. Initially choose two children at opposite sides of the parachute to let go of their grip and run underneath the chute to swap places as it rises. They need to look carefully and cross as quickly as possible. If a child remains underneath, just allow the chute to drift slowly down so that the child can crawl out. Once you and the children are more confident in the way the parachute moves, choose four or six children to swap places. Continue until all the children have had a turn at crossing over, or everyone's arms are tired.

Build in a calming-down period after this exciting play. Everyone lies on the floor with the chute over their legs and lower body; the edge of the chute can be under their armpits. Use this opportunity for chatting about the children's experiences, how they felt under the chute, did they notice the light or colour underneath the parachute: talking while lying down without being able to see the 'talker' is probably a new experience to most children.

Story Characters

One of the best ways to begin any simple dramatic play activity is to start with a familiar story. Stories give children the opportunity to be animals, monsters, inanimate objects or other people. Adults may need to model this by pretending to be characters themselves. Remember that an important element of the children's learning will be mimicking what you do – so overcome embarrassment if necessary to pretend to be a horse in a field, an owl in a tree, etc. Start simply and informally and build towards more elaborate storylines and interpretations.

Goldilocks and the Three Bears is a well-known story that lends itself well to role-play. As the story is told the children will probably need very little guidance in acting out the roles. Try adding extra characters if more children want to take part. These characters can be incorporated as Goldilocks walks through the woods and meets people and animals on the way. The children might also like to alter the ending so that Goldilocks cooks the bears' breakfast, or invites them to her house for a tea party to say sorry, etc.

There are literally hundreds of traditional tales you can use from all over the world. Begin, as we've suggested, by improvising familiar ones and progress towards lesser-known and/or more complex stories. Once the children are familiar with them they can adapt and change them as they like.

A modern favourite is Jill Murphy's *On The Way Home*. A child falls off the swing at the playground and cuts her knee. On the way home to Mummy she meets lots of friends and to each one she tells a different story of how she came by her injury. Children love to invent what else could have happened to the girl – acting out the tale is a bonus!

Small World Play

Small world play equipment gives children the opportunity for role-play in miniature, and is suitable for solitary play as well as parallel and cooperative play. Also, some children don't feel comfortable with big body movement, and so small world play can offer them a greater freedom of expression. Giving children such freedom lets them develop their curiosity, expressiveness and observational and manipulative skills. Often it's better if this is not teacher-led: just have the resources available for children to get on and use for themselves.

There are some wonderful miniature play items available in toy shops and through educational suppliers, involving airports, pirates, farmyards, trains, circuses and dolls' houses, with small-scale figures from different countries, including Africa, Asia, Europe and Japan, etc. You do not need to provide perfect replicas: let the children improvise.

Add some green, black/grey, brown, printed and patterned fabric. This will inspire a child's imagination and become hills, fields, lawns and gardens, roads, runways, tents, etc. Boxes can be painted to become buildings, such as houses, flats, factories and offices. Building bricks can become harbours, railway tracks and roadways. Lollipop sticks, pegs and spent matches can be use to indicate the edges of runways, or fences on a farm or zoo.

Remember to keep a light touch: let the children create their miniature worlds of play.

Acting Out Rhymes

Acting out nursery rhymes is very simple and such fun. Shy children will often sing along and eventually want to join in, once they understand how enjoyable and unthreatening the activity is.

The idea is to create little scenarios. Rhymes only last a few minutes, enabling all the children to 'have a go' if they wish. There is no real need to 'act'; they can just take part without pressure, for example during circle time or a music session, or at the end of story time, etc.

For example: with a group of children seated sing 'Miss Polly had a Dolly'. Instead of doing the actions as usual, ask if anyone would like to be 'Miss Polly' or 'Mr Jolly' and a doctor (male or female), and, with a doll, do the song. Occasionally I have had a group of children who want a telephone, bag, hat and prescription to complete the 'show', but this is not essential. As the 'actors' sing their particular parts the children sitting can sing along as well. Also roles can change or you can sing other songs with different 'actors' so that every child who wants to can have a share of the limelight.

Number Acts

Acting out number rhymes to create little scenarios is so easy and simple to do: either sing the original song or alter it. For example, sing 'Five Currant Buns in a Baker's Shop', and then act it out. Five children volunteer to be cakes, and you also need a baker and people to 'buy' the cakes. The five 'buns' stand in a line with the baker in the shop. Along comes a customer who chooses a bun, pays the baker and walks away with the bun. Repeat the scenario until there are no buns left. This simple activity can be extended further by creating a pretend baker's shop with children as the baker, customers, a delivery person and so on.

Alternatively, using 'Five Little Men in a Flying Saucer', five children hold hands and 'fly' around the room while the other children sing 'Five little men in a flying saucer flew round (name of preschool) one day / They looked left and right and really liked the sight / So one of them decided to stay.' One of the 'flying' children then drops hands with the others and joins the group of singing children on the floor. Repeat until no one is left in the flying saucer.

Mimed Stories

This activity uses your voice, body sounds and mime – but no words – to tell a story. Explain to the children what you will be doing, then exaggerate your movements, move slowly and use as many sounds as you can so that the story is easier to follow. Start with a familiar story and one that is short and has only one main character (e.g. *The Very Hungry Caterpillar* by Eric Carle, or *Mr Gumpy's Outing* by John Burningham).

Preparation is the key, so go through the mime beforehand. Is it simple enough; can you 'see' and 'feel' the story through your actions? Once you've shown the children, chat with them about what they thought was happening in the tale. Initially you may want to use a few props or give the mime a title to allow the children to 'tune in' to the mime.

This type of activity can cause lots of frustration because it is very difficult not to talk while miming, but it creates lots of laughter, especially as actions and sound effects often have alternative meanings that look and sound funny.

Work with the children to develop other stories in this way, adapting already-known tales and making up new stories to be mimed. For example: Sally went for a walk. She went along the path to the river. She heard the birds singing and squirrels running through the leaves under the trees. Then the wind blew through the trees and it started to rain, so Sally decided to go home, jumping in lots of puddles as she went. The front door was closed when Sally got home. She rang the bell, so happy to be home and out of the rain.

Puppets

Puppets come in many varieties: finger, hand or glove, stick or rod, string, shadow, or as ventriloquist dummies. The simplest for young children to use are finger puppets. They are also the easiest to make in order to enhance a rhyme, story or imaginative play activities. Usually finger puppets are made to cover one finger, but they can be used with the index and middle fingers too.

Children can make the body of the puppet, as almost any coloured or painted shape can be turned into a finger puppet immediately. Attach a ring of paper or card to the back of the cut-out shape, allowing the whole shape to move. Alternatively, make a walking puppet by cutting two holes towards the base of the object large enough for the index and middle fingers to protrude as 'legs'. Or stick a rectangular piece of card to the back of the cut-out shape so that the index or middle finger can fit in the 'pouch', enabling the puppet to dance about (adults may need to do most of these 'additions').

Alternatively, rectangular shapes (approx. 4–5cm x 7cm) can be cut out beforehand, and two pieces stapled together with one narrower side left open for the finger. The children may make them into people or animals or decorate them brightly to aid their play.

Story Box

This is like a themed feelie box (see Idea 71), filled with items featuring in stories that you know the children are familiar with (e.g. a teddy, which appears in *Goldilocks and the Three Bears*, *Peace at Last* by Jill Murphy, *Bear Hunt* by various authors, *This is the Bear* series by Sarah Hayes, etc.). Make sure that you and the children are comfortable and familiar with the items in the box: it's no use putting in a plastic crocodile if you don't know or don't feel you can make up a story featuring one.

Have the children pick items from the box to make up a group story, which may be similar to the story the children already know. Start simple, so for instance put in three different-sized bowls to use as a basis for the Goldilocks story (or a variation of it). This gives children a starting point and helps prevent them from feeling frightened of getting stuck or giving a wrong answer, but you also already have flexibility within a structure insofar as the activity lends itself to variants of the original tale and, in time, much more original tales. Use your judgement in using other items that don't conventionally go into the story. Feed the children's creativity . . . And steer away from silliness.

Storyboards

One of our favourite activities with preschoolers is *telling* stories, not reading a story from a book. The fact that there is no book to hide behind and nothing between you and the children creates a closer relationship with the group. However, this requires greater confidence on your part.

There are many ways to bridge the gap between reading a storybook and telling a tale, and so to increase your level of confidence to 'go it alone'. One idea is the use of a storyboard. This is simply a board on which a story is told. The principle is similar to reusable sticker albums or Fuzzy Felt. Pictures are drawn or cut from old books and need to be prepared and numbered in advance. Pins, Blu-tack or magnets add the pictures as you tell the story.

The board can be cork (with drawing pins), a magnetic noticeboard (using magnets or self-adhesive magnetic tape), a stiff plastic sheet or sheet of card covered with sticky-back plastic (and Blu-tack), or a board covered with felt (using self-adhesive Velcro or coarse sandpaper). We have also used a cushion and dressmaking pins, so almost anything goes!

There are advantages and disadvantages to each type of board. Some attachments take extra preparation but are more durable. Pins or Blu-tack are fiddly when in the flow of your story and can cause damage to the pictures when used regularly. Magnets can wipe information from cassette tapes or phones, etc. and need to be carefully stored.

Try out ideas before telling a story with the children. Subsequently, let the children use storyboards for themselves (although clearly pins must then be avoided).

Feelings Board

- The children draw favourite people, objects, colours and shapes, or cut out pictures and images from magazines, comics or catalogues that have good associations and make them feel happy. Each child can create a montage on a 'happy thoughts' page with a smiley face at the top, or incorporate everything into a group wall display.

- Do the same with things that make the children sad – colours, images, shapes, pictures, etc. that they don't like, want or need. Have an unhappy thoughts page with a down-turned smile on which children stick images to make a montage of sad/bad feelings.

Exploring feelings, sharing experiences, linking feelings with colours and images and *then manipulating them* is one way of developing children's emotional intelligence. This is the potential we all possess to connect thoughts, feelings and physical responses to our life experiences and to develop strategies to modify and control how we feel. This goes hand-in-hand with an increasing ability to empathize with others and have insights into how they experience the world. That's why it is important to explore negative as well as positive emotions. Emotional intelligence isn't about avoiding or suppressing the negative, but developing creative ways of dealing with it.

Experiences and Feelings

- Having created montages or a group wall display (see Idea 98), lead a discussion about what makes you and the children grin from ear to ear, what makes you laugh, chuckle, or smile 'quietly' – they're all happy feelings but some are 'happier' thoughts than others. Explore the things that make us all happy.

- Depending on the way the images make us feel, perhaps extend the activity to involve a small group and draw a bar chart (graph) with large grin, small smile, laughing faces, etc. on the base line, and choose a few pictures, sounds and colours to go on the vertical. Ask the children which gives them the biggest smile and record their names on the chart, and see which 'item' is the most popular or the one which gives the most BIG grins.

- Depending on the age, ability and interest of the children, discuss whether the same things make boys happy, smile or laugh more, or whether girls like certain activities more than boys.

- Again, extend the activity to sad things and guide discussion of how sadness might be changed to happiness. Using familiar concrete examples of change from negative to positive paves the way for allowing children to deal more capably with their feelings.

Feelings and Responses

- Listen to sounds you make.

- Listen to yourself walking – listen to yourself breathing.

- Listen to yourself running – listen to your breathing: has the pattern changed? Are you breathing more quickly, slowly, quietly, noisily?

- Listen to a partner/other friends.

- Can you alter the sounds, make them louder, quieter?

- What makes you breathe more quickly? Notice that you can control your own breathing.

- Start to whisper, saying the word whisper – and get louder and louder.

- Start to laugh quietly, saying laughing – get louder and louder.

- Start to sing quietly, using the word singing – get louder and louder.

- Do the sounds remind you of anything? How do they make you feel inside? Do they make you happy or sad? Do they make you feel like keeping still or dancing about?

- If you can't black out your room, try making a 'tent' with dark fabric and sit inside. Watch the movements you make: do you move differently in the dark?

- How does it make you feel in the dark? Is it different if you have a torch?

- Put coloured Perspex over the torchlight. Do you move or talk differently with the different colours? Do you have a sound for green light – would you have a different one for red?

- The torchlight can make shadows. Can you make the shadows dance? How does it make you feel?

- Working in a group of three or four, whisper to one friend. How do you feel when you know you're telling a secret? How do your friends feel, not knowing the secret?

NB: Use these activities sparingly or in short bursts with the children. Little ones especially can become overwhelmed and emotionally overloaded if too much is demanded of them at once.